Bay Area
Mountain Bike Trails

45 Mountain Bike Rides
Throughout the San Francisco Bay Area

by
Conrad J. Boisvert

Penngrove Publications
P.O. Box 1017
Penngrove, CA 94951

To Jean

Library of Congress Catalog Card Number 93-085913
International Standard Book Number 0-9621694-5-5

Cover photograph by Bob Morris
Taken on Mt. Tamalpais, off Panoramic Highway
Cyclists: Conrad Boisvert and Jean Newton

Photographs in the book were taken by Conrad Boisvert

Printed in the United States of America
Lithocraft, Inc.
424 Aviation Boulevard
Santa Rosa, California

First printing, November 1993
Second printing, September 1995

Penngrove Publications
P.O. Box 1017
Penngrove, CA 94951

TABLE OF CONTENTS

ACKNOWLEDGMENTS

Special thanks and recognition need to go to the many dedicated park rangers and public servants who work endlessly to make visits to our public land enjoyable. State parks, county parks, open space preserves, and national parks and recreational areas all need to be cared for in order to ensure that they survive and remain undefiled. Only through the efforts of park administrators and rangers, who often work for substandard pay to do what they believe in, can this be assured.

On a personal level, I want to express my deepest appreciation for the support of my family. My mother, Helen, and my children, Judie, Charles, and Steve, all deserve my heartfelt thanks for their continuous encouragement. Special thanks goes to Jean Newton for her warmth, her many suggestions, and her time spent as a companion on many of the rides for this book. Others who have helped me in selecting the rides and doing them with me include: Bob Godwin, Dennis Vanata, Richard Wong, Kathy Picard, and Klaus Schumann.

Thanks go to my publisher, Phyllis Neumann, for her confidence and for her patience in resolving the many issues which naturally arise in a production of this kind. Linda Cardone, for her help in putting the book together, and Bob Morris, for his fine cover photo, also deserve my deepest thanks.

EXPLORE BAY AREA TRAILS
ON A MOUNTAIN BIKE

Rich geographical diversity and a mild climate make the San Francisco Bay Area a very special place to live. From its fog-shrouded coastal forests populated with ancient redwoods to its rugged chaparral, so characteristic of its inland mountains, the Bay Area has a fascinating variety of terrain. Blessed with a mild Mediterranean climate, few places can match the Bay Area for its multitude of year-round outdoor activities. Despite the ever-increasing population density of the entire region, it is still easy to get away to remote mountain trails and to get close to nature. In the hills and mountains which ring the Bay Area can be found numerous parks and public lands ideal for the rapidly-growing sport of mountain biking.

State parks, county parks, and regional open space preserves form the backbone of the public-access lands with trails for biking. National parks, monuments and recreation areas within the Bay Area add to these to create a decidedly wide range of choices. While narrow trails in all areas are oftentimes not open to bicycles, fire roads usually are. It is important for responsible riders to be cognizant and to respect the laws and rules of each area. Riding on illegal trails is not only against the law, but violates the rules of common sense, as well.

Stretching from Santa Rosa in the north to Gilroy in the south, any city in the Bay Area has mountain biking within easy reach. From Mt. Tamalpais in Marin, where the mountain biking concept was first developed, to Henry Coe State Park in Morgan Hill, where continuous improvement in bike technology takes place, courtesy of the folks at Specialized Bicycles, the Bay Area has historic significance for the sport.

While many trails exist in close proximity to the large population centers of the region, the best riding is often found farther away. Few places get more remote than the southern section of Henry Coe near Gilroy or the little-known Morgan Territory near Livermore. Few places have more miles of trails to explore than the public land surrounding majestic Mt. Tamalpais.

The appeal of mountain biking is almost obvious. How else is it possible to cover the many miles of trails as quickly and as easily as on a bike? By foot, a ten-mile hike can take 3-4 hours, whereas on a mountain bike, it is easily done in 1-2 hours. The challenges of mastering the techniques of mountain biking add to its allure.

While there is considerable dispute about the ability of bikes to share the trails with hikers and equestrians, common courtesy and consideration for others on the part of all mountain bikers will ensure that harmonious coexistence will prevail.

REGIONS OF THE BAY AREA

The South Bay   *Cupertino to Gilroy*

The South Bay region is centered around San Jose. Nearby is the rugged terrain of Grant Ranch in the foothills of Mt. Hamilton, the chaparral-covered mountains of Sierra Azul Open Space near Los Gatos, and the popular (and crowded) Los Gatos Creek Trail. Farther afield from San Jose are the primitive and remote Henry Coe State Park, the redwood forests and steep mountains at The Forest of Nisene Marks and Big Basin, and the single-track trails of Wilder Ranch and Soquel Demonstration Forest.

The San Francisco Peninsula   *San Francisco to Palo Alto*

Mountain biking in the San Francisco Peninsula region is available primarily in the vast amount of public land administered by the Midpeninsula Regional Open Space District. Arastradero, Monte Bello, Fremont Older, Long Ridge, Russian Ridge, Skyline Ridge, Windy Hill, and Purisima Redwoods are examples of open space preserves in the Santa Cruz Mountains that are open to mountain biking. In many cases, it is possible to link together trails in adjacent preserves in order to create mountain bike routes of impressive lengths. While the terrain is usually quite steep and the hills are quite high, the deep forests provide refreshing relief even on the hottest days of summer.

The East Bay   *Carquinez Strait to Milpitas*

Whereas the East Bay is usually the hottest and driest of all Bay Area regions in the summer months, its beauty in the spring and fall is unrivaled. In springtime, when the grass-covered slopes are green from the winter moisture and the creeks are flowing with mountain run-off, the area is hard to beat. The cooling days of the fall bring the golden colors of the season to their peak brilliance. Although the East Bay hills are generally not as high as those along the coast, Mt. Diablo remains one of the tallest in the entire Bay Area and its trails can challenge even the best riders.

The North Bay   *Marin and Sonoma Counties*

It is no accident that the North Bay was the birthplace of the mountain bicycle. The endless miles of trails around Mt. Tamalpais absolutely demanded that a rugged all-terrain bike be developed. The scenery from the mountain trails, as well as from the trails of the Marin Headlands, are unsurpassed. At each turn, views of the vast Pacific Ocean, Sausalito, Angel Island, and the magnificent San Francisco skyline, continue to impress no matter how many times they are seen.

THE SAN FRANCISCO BAY AREA

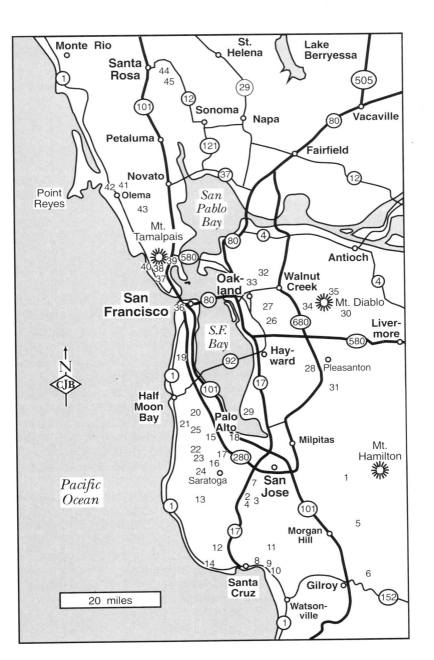

HOW TO USE THIS BOOK

Ride Parameters

At the beginning of each ride description is a short list of ride parameters. These are intended to give you a quick summary of that particular ride and to permit you to sort through the rides to find the ones that best suit your own personal needs.

Difficulty Rating — reflects the overall difficulty of the ride, in terms of the general physical effort needed. There are three levels: *easy*, *moderate*, and *difficult*. The rating for a particular ride usually depends upon the distance and the total elevation gain of the ride and is also affected by the steepness of the grades.

Skill Level — refers to the technical mountain biking skills required to do the ride: beginner, intermediate, and advanced. Rides needing *beginner* skills usually have wide trails and relatively gentle grades. Those requiring *advanced* skills normally have narrow and steep trails and may also have tight switchbacks to contend with.

Elevation Gain — combines the elevation gains of all the climbing required. For example, climbing two hills, each with 500 feet of elevation gain, would result in 1,000 feet of total elevation gain.

Total Distance — indicates the total length of the ride.

Off-Road Distance — the number of miles of off-road riding in the ride. This consists of both dirt roads and paved and unpaved trails.

Riding Time — gives an indication of how much time to budget for the ride. Keep in mind, however, that this does not include extended stops for sightseeing, eating, and resting. The riding time usually assumes a moderate pace of about 4-7 miles per hour.

Total Calories — estimates the total amount of energy burned. This is based upon an average calorie burn rate of about 400 calories/hour on a flat unpaved road at about 12 miles/hour and about 900 calories/hour on a hill climb with a grade of about 8% and with a speed of about 4 miles/hour. Some variations will naturally occur for differences in individual riders and for external factors, like extra weight carried on the bike.

About the Ride

This section contains a general description of the ride, along with any interesting background information for the area. The general route to be followed is explained, although the details are covered in the *Mile Markers* section.

The conditions of trails and roads, expected car traffic, and general terrain are also briefly described to permit you to quickly determine if the ride is right for you.

Elevation Profile

An elevation profile for each ride provides a detailed graph of the required hill climbs. It not only previews the climbing for you, but can be a useful reference to take with you on your ride, since it can help prepare you for the hills you will encounter along the way. Grades (in percent) for significant hill climbs are often indicated on the diagrams. A 10% grade is one that has about 500 vertical feet of elevation gain for each mile of distance.

Starting Point

The exact place to start the ride is described, along with detailed directions explaining how to get there. In general, rides are started at locations where free parking is readily available and where refreshments can be purchased for either before or after your ride. Typically, starting locations are easily recognizable places with public restrooms, making them convenient for groups of people meeting to ride together.

Mile Markers

Directions for the route are described, along with the total ride distance for each item. You don't necessarily need to have a cycle computer to follow the mile markers, since they come at frequent intervals and you will quickly learn to estimate distances accurately enough. The markers indicate the required turns to take in order to follow the route, as well as point out special sights and features of the ride that you might otherwise miss.

Map

Each ride has a map associated with it indicating the route. In general, however, the map is not necessary for following the route, since detailed directions are included in the *Mile Markers* section. For clarity, the starting point of each ride is indicated on the map by an asterisk enclosed by a circle.✹

The South Bay

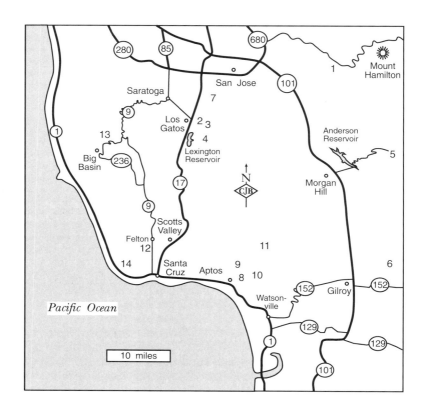

280 85 680

1

Mount
Hamilton

San Jose

101

Saratoga

7

9

Los
Gatos 2 3

13 4

Lexington
Reservoir

Big
Basin 236

Anderson
Reservoir

5

1

N
CJB

Morgan
Hill

17

9

Scotts
Valley

Felton 11

12

14 Santa
Cruz Aptos 9

8 10

6

Watson-
ville 152 Gilroy 152

Pacific Ocean

129

1

129

10 miles

101

1

San Jose
Grant Ranch County Park

Region: *South Bay*
Difficulty Rating: *Difficult*
Skill Level: *Intermediate*
Elevation Gain: *1900 feet*

Total Distance: *16 miles*
Off-Road Distance: *16 miles*
Riding Time: *3 hours*
Total Calories: *1200*

About the Ride

In the foothills of Mount Hamilton, just a short distance from central San Jose, lies the former Grant Ranch, once an operating cattle ranch. Now a county park, Grant Ranch offers challenging mountain biking along wide fire roads through pastures populated with grazing livestock. While the park is not entirely open to biking, this route will lead you around that portion of the park that is.

After a short 1-mile stretch of trail leading away from the parking lot, a rather steep section gets the heart pounding. Once past Eagle Lake, more climbing along Digger Pine Trail and Bohnhoff Trail leads to Mount Hamilton Road, across which the trail continues. Cañada de Pala Trail leads through a high meadow and to an old line shack formerly used by ranch hands. After this, it's nearly all downhill back to park headquarters, from which the route began.

Almost 2,000 feet of climbing on some rather steep trails makes this ride a difficult one. The trails are wide and relatively smooth though, so intermediate-level skills are all that are necessary.

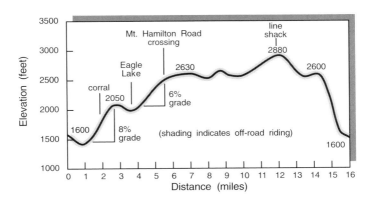

Starting Point

Grant Ranch County Park is located on Mt. Hamilton Road, east of San Jose. To get there, take the Alum Rock Avenue exit off Highway 680 and proceed east for about 2 miles. Turn right on Mt. Hamilton Road and continue for about 8 miles to Grant Ranch. Enter at the main entrance and go all the way through and to the left side where the visitor center and trailhead are located.

Mile Markers

0.0 Proceed EAST from the parking area. Go past two livestock gates to the Hotel Trail.

0.3 Bear RIGHT onto Lower Hotel Trail and begin descent.

1.0 Barn Trail intersection on the right side.

1.6 Livestock gate.

1.8 Continue STRAIGHT through the corral.

1.9 Steep uphill section.

2.3 Trail intersection on the left side.

3.5 Eagle Lake on the right side. Bear LEFT and descend into the canyon. Begin Digger Pine Trail.

4.6 Turn LEFT onto Bohnhoff Trail — steep uphill.

5.5 Continue STRAIGHT across Mt. Hamilton Road and get on Cañada de Pala Trail.

6.0 Yerba Buena Trail intersection on the left side.

7.3 Continue STRAIGHT at Los Huecos Trail intersection on the left side.

8.5 Bear LEFT to stay on Cañada de Pala Trail.

10.2 Pass old line shack on the left and then bear RIGHT to get on Pala Seca Trail.

12.3 Continue STRAIGHT at the trail intersection to get back on Cañada de Pala Trail.

13.5 Turn RIGHT onto Los Huecos Trail. Steep descent.

14.4 Gate.

15.3 Reservoir — turn LEFT to stay on trail.

15.6 Continue STRAIGHT through parking lot and turn RIGHT onto Mt. Hamilton Road.

16.0 Turn LEFT into park entrance.

16.4 End of the ride at the parking lot.

Further Information

Grant Ranch County Park: (408) 358-3741

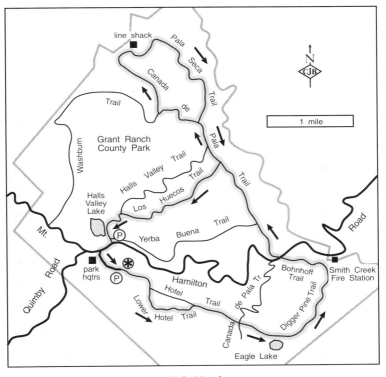

Ride No. 1

2 Los Gatos
St. Joseph's Hill

Region: *South Bay*	**Total Distance**: *6 miles*
Difficulty Rating: *Moderate*	**Off-Road Distance**: *5 miles*
Skill Level: *Intermediate*	**Riding Time:** *1-2 hours*
Elevation Gain: *700 feet*	**Total Calories**: *300*

About the Ride

Formerly owned by the California Society of the Province of Jesus, St. Joseph's Hill Open Space Preserve is situated near central Los Gatos and is quite popular with local cyclists and hikers. While the trails are very steep in places, the ride is only rated as a moderate-level ride because it is not very long and climbs only about 700 feet. Intermediate riders may find it more difficult than they expect because of the steepness.

The route begins in Los Gatos at Los Gatos High School where there is plenty of parking. Once you leave central Los Gatos, the Los Gatos Creek Trail will lead you to Lexington Dam and Reservoir. Just past the dam can be found the trailhead leading into St. Joseph's Hill Open Space. Steep climbing will take you to the top of the hill, from which there are sweeping views of the South Bay and Lexington Reservoir. The trail then leads back down off the hill and out the north exit of the preserve and back to the high school.

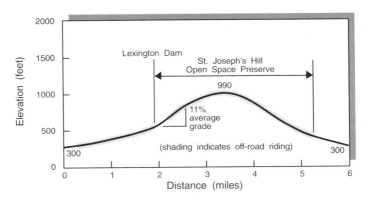

Starting Point

Start the ride at Los Gatos High School in Los Gatos. Take the Saratoga Avenue (Highway 9) exit off Highway 17 and go east on Saratoga Avenue to the intersection with Los Gatos Boulevard. Turn right on Los Gatos Boulevard (which becomes East Main Street) and follow it for about ½-mile to the high school, located on the right side. Park in the rear of the school or anywhere nearby.

Mile Markers

0.0   Proceed WEST on East Main Street, heading toward central Los Gatos.

0.2   Turn LEFT just before the Highway 17 overcrossing and get on Los Gatos Creek Trail.

1.8   Bear LEFT across a small bridge and then climb a steep section to get to the top of the Lexington Dam.

2.0   At the top of the dam, turn LEFT onto Alma Bridge Road.

2.2   Turn LEFT to enter St. Joseph's Hill Open Space Preserve at a gate marked "SJ03." Begin a steep climb immediately.

2.7   Turn RIGHT at the junction for Jones Trail. From the ridge along this section, you can see the Sierra Azul Open Space Preserve across the canyon.

3.3   Turn RIGHT off Jones Trail and climb up towards St. Joseph's Hill.

3.4   Turn RIGHT onto the double-track and proceed around the top of the hill. Notice the old vineyard posts on the left from the time when the Novitiate Winery grew its own grapes.

3.6   The trail becomes a narrow single-track as Los Gatos High School and the winery come into view below.

4.1   Continue STRAIGHT at the junction with Jones Trail.

4.3   Bear RIGHT at trail junction.

4.5   Turn RIGHT onto Jones Trail.

4.9   Walk your bike through the section with the warning signs.

5.4   Continue STRAIGHT at the gate, exit the preserve and get on Jones Road.

5.6   Turn LEFT onto College Road.

6.0   Turn RIGHT onto East Main Street.

6.2   End of the ride at Los Gatos High School.

Further Information

Midpeninsula Regional Open Space District: (415) 949-5500

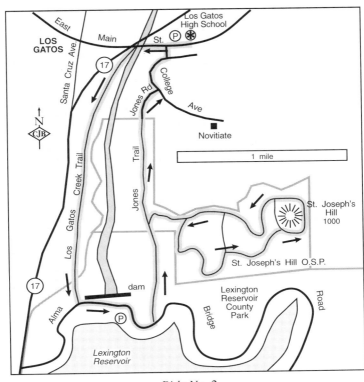

Ride No. 2

The trail into St. Joseph's Hill.

3 Los Gatos

Sierra Azul Open Space Preserve #1

Region: *South Bay*
Difficulty Rating: *Difficult*
Skill Level: *Advanced*
Elevation Gain: *2300 feet*

Total Distance: *12 miles*
Off-Road Distance: *8 miles*
Riding Time: *2-3 hours*
Total Calories: *1200*

About the Ride

The Sierra Azul (Spanish for "blue mountains") Open Space Preserve is situated in the mountains above Lexington Reservoir near Los Gatos and stretches all the way to Mount Umunhum, above San Jose. Fire roads lead through the preserve and climb along scrub-covered ridges to elevations as high as 2,600 feet where there are panoramic views of the Santa Clara Valley and the Santa Cruz Mountains. The ride is strenuous and has some steep climbs and descents. Though the trails are wide, there is plenty of challenge for even the most experienced riders.

The route begins in Los Gatos and leads through quiet residential neighborhoods along a steady climb on Kennedy Road. The trailhead into Sierra Azul is located at the top of the hill on Kennedy Road. After a brief flat section at the beginning, the fire road then climbs steeply as it leads you to the top of the ridge. An even steeper descent off the ridge takes you to a major trail intersection. At this point, you will turn and then follow along a challenging single-track trail through some dense woods and then exit the preserve at Lexington Reservoir. A short stretch along the road takes you to the Lexington Dam, at which point you will get on Los Gatos Creek Trail for the return to town.

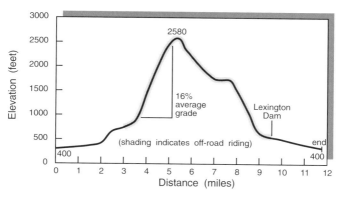

Starting Point

Start the ride at Los Gatos High School in Los Gatos. Take the Saratoga Avenue (Highway 9) exit off Highway 17 and go east on Saratoga Avenue to the intersection with Los Gatos Boulevard. Turn right on Los Gatos Boulevard (which becomes East Main Street) and follow it for about ½-mile to the high school, located on the right side. Park in the rear of the school or anywhere nearby.

Mile Markers

0.0 Proceed EAST on East Main Street, heading away from Los Gatos.

0.5 Continue STRAIGHT at the intersection with Saratoga Avenue on the left side.

0.7 Turn RIGHT onto Kennedy Road.

3.0 Turn RIGHT and enter into Sierra Azul Open Space Preserve at the crest of Kennedy Road.

3.6 Steep climbing begins.

5.6 Summit — 2,580-foot elevation.

5.7 Bear RIGHT at trail split.

5.8 Steep descent begins.

6.6 Continue STRAIGHT at trail junction on the left.

7.0 Turn RIGHT at major junction where four trails come together.

7.3 Continue past gate. Begin narrow and steep single-track section.

8.8 Exit the preserve and turn RIGHT onto Alma Bridge Road.

9.6 Turn RIGHT onto Los Gatos Creek Trail just beyond the boathouse at the top of Lexington Dam.

11.3 At the end of the trail, turn RIGHT onto East Main Street.

11.7 Back at Los Gatos High School.

Further Information

Midpeninsula Regional Open Space District: (415) 949-5500

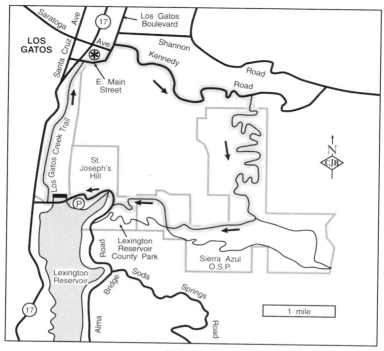

Ride No. 3

Along the ridgeline in Sierra Azul.

4 Los Gatos
Sierra Azul Open Space Preserve #2

Region: *South Bay*
Difficulty Rating: *Difficult*
Skill Level: *Advanced*
Elevation Gain: *2700 feet*

Total Distance: *13 miles*
Off-Road Distance: *11 miles*
Riding Time: *2-3 hours*
Total Calories: *1600*

About the Ride

This is the second of two rides in the Sierra Azul Open Space Preserve, located near Los Gatos. Like the first, this ride has some very steep sections and climbs to a rather high elevation (2,800 feet, in this case). The trails are not well-marked, but are easy to follow since there aren't very many of them. It would be hard to get lost. Summers are hot and dry, so be sure to bring along plenty of water.

The route leads around the southeastern section of the preserve, an area less traveled but no less beautiful than the other. From Lexington Dam, the starting point, a short stretch along isolated Alma Bridge Road leads around the shoreline of the reservoir to the trailhead. Once in the preserve, the fire road immediately climbs steeply as it leads you to the top of the mountain. At the far eastern edge of the preserve are views of the Mount Umunhum radar station. On the way back from the eastern extreme are some spectacular views into the Santa Clara Valley toward San Jose. A steep descent along the fire road is followed by a winding single-track through the forest in the lower elevations of the preserve. Back on Alma Bridge Road, it is but a short hop back to the dam.

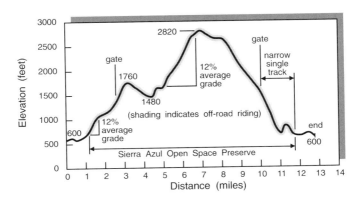

Starting Point

The ride starts at Lexington Dam, near Los Gatos. To get there, take Highway 17 toward Santa Cruz and get off just past Los Gatos at Alma Bridge Road. Follow the road a short distance to the dam, where there is plenty of public parking.

Mile Markers

0.0   Proceed EAST on Alma Bridge Road, heading away from Highway 17.

0.8   Continue STRAIGHT at first gate into Sierra Azul on the left side.

1.1   Turn LEFT to enter Sierra Azul at gate marked "SA21." Begin to climb steeply immediately.

2.6   Pass through gate marked "SA23."

3.6   Turn RIGHT at major trail junction connecting four trails.

6.4   Views of Mount Umunhum radar station off to the right

6.7   Turn LEFT at trail intersection. Straight ahead is the park boundary and private property.

7.0   Great views of the Santa Clara Valley.

7.2   Continue STRAIGHT at the trail intersection on the left side.

8.2   Turn LEFT at trail intersection. Begin very steep descent.

9.6   Turn RIGHT at major 4-way trail intersection.

10.0   Continue past the gate. Narrow single-track begins.

11.7   Continue past the gate at the end of the trail and turn RIGHT onto Alma Bridge Road.

12.5   End of the ride back at Lexington Dam.

Further Information

Midpeninsula Regional Open Space District: (415) 949-5500

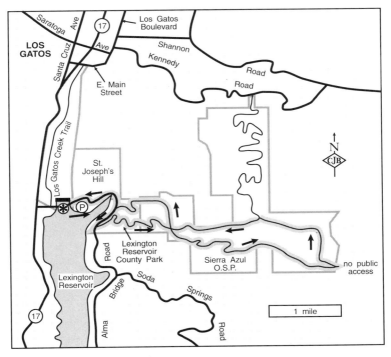

Ride No. 4

5 Morgan Hill
Henry Coe State Park —
Middle Ridge Loop

Region: *South Bay*
Difficulty Rating: *Difficult*
Skill Level: *Advanced*
Elevation Gain: *2100 feet*

Total Distance: *10 miles*
Off-Road Distance: *10 miles*
Riding Time: *2 hours*
Total Calories: *1000*

About the Ride

About 12 miles east of Morgan Hill in Southern Santa Clara County lies Henry Coe State Park, one of the largest and most remote of all the parks in the Bay Area. Its remoteness is also part of its mystique. Unusual wildlife is plentiful — it is not at all uncommon to see wild turkeys, golden eagles, and wild pigs. Snakes and poison oak are common too, so be extremely careful when visiting the park.

This ride leads you around the northern section of the park, the most popular area. Park headquarters is the starting point. Be sure to check in with the ranger before you begin your ride to get current trail conditions and bicycle rules. A brief visit will also acquaint you with the park and help you to get the most out of your tour. The route leads on a wide fire road away from the ranger station and climbs a short hill to the monument for Henry Coe, the former owner of the ranch. After a small drop and another short climb, you will turn onto Middle Ridge Trail. The steep descent along the narrow single-track has many switchbacks and offers plenty of challenge for anyone. At the bottom, at Poverty Flat, there is a stream crossing and then a wide fire road climbs steeply back to the ranger station, from where you began.

Starting Point

Start the ride at park headquarters in Henry Coe State Park. Take Highway 101 south to Morgan Hill and get off at east Dunne Avenue. Follow East Dunne Avenue east for about 12 miles up into the mountains. At the end of the road is the park, where there is a nominal fee for parking and day use.

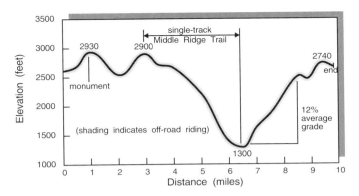

Mile Markers

0.0   Get on the fire road across from the ranger station and begin climbing.

0.5   Turn LEFT at the junction of two fire roads and begin climbing toward the monument.

1.0   Bear LEFT at the junction with the trail to Frog Lake to stay on the fire road.

2.2   Frog Lake is to the right.

2.7   Crest — begin downhill section.

3.0   Turn RIGHT at the summit and head toward Frog Lake on single-track trail.

3.2   Bear LEFT at trail junction — Frog Lake is to the right.

4.0   Begin steep and narrow descent for 2.5 miles — be careful.

4.4   Bear LEFT at trail split and head toward Poverty Flat.

6.4   Stream crossing.

6.5   Cross stream and turn RIGHT onto the fire road. Begin climbing.

8.1   Continue STRAIGHT at the intersection with the fire road on the left side.

9.8   End of the ride back at park headquarters.

Further Information

Henry Coe State Park: (408) 779-2728

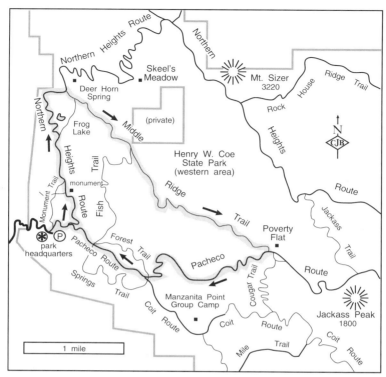

Ride No. 5

The historic Coe Ranch.

6 Gilroy

Henry Coe State Park — Southern Section

Region: *South Bay*	**Total Distance:** *16 miles*
Difficulty Rating: *Difficult*	**Off-Road Distance:** *16 miles*
Skill Level: *Beginner*	**Riding Time:** *3 hours*
Elevation Gain: *2300 feet*	**Total Calories:** *1400*

About the Ride

Henry Coe State Park lies about 12 miles east of Morgan Hill and Gilroy, in the southernmost part of Santa Clara County. The former operating ranch of Henry Coe, the park today is one of the largest state parks in northern California and continues to grow as new lands are acquired on a fairly regular basis.

The southern section of the park, not nearly as well-known as the northern section, is the focus of this ride. There is a way into the park near the once-famous Gilroy Hot Springs on Gilroy Hot Springs Road. No services are available in this part of the park, so be sure to come with adequate water and snacks.

The ride follows a simple out-and-back route to pristine Kelly Lake along wide fire roads. The start of the ride is flat as it follows along Coyote Creek. In the early part of the ride, the old buildings of Gilroy Hot Springs can be seen across the creek. About 3 miles into the ride, the fire road climbs as it leads away from the creek and toward the ridge. At the top, the trail then follows along the ridge line and offers spectacular views in both directions. The descent is an easy one and is followed by a short stretch along another creek leading to Kelly Lake.

The trails are well-marked and easy to follow. While there is substantial climbing, the grades are not terribly steep and no special riding skills are needed. Summers can be hot and dry, so be prepared and avoid the hottest days. Springtime is the best time to visit when creeks are flowing and the hills are green.

Starting Point

Take Highway 101 south toward Gilroy. Get off at Leavesley Road and follow it east about 2 miles. Turn left onto New Avenue and then right onto Roop Road, which becomes Gilroy Hot Springs Road. At the end of the road is an unobtrusive fire road leading into the park on the right side of the road. You can park anywhere along the road.

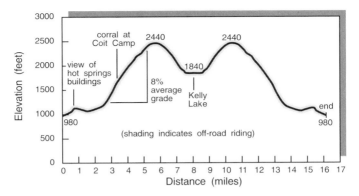

Mile Markers

0.0 Proceed EAST into the park on the fire road located on the right side of the roadway.

0.1 Bear LEFT at trail split and enter Henry Coe State Park. Cross stream immediately.

0.7 Views of Gilroy Hot Springs buildings on the left side across Coyote Creek.

2.2 Begin climbing.

3.3 Coit Camp — corral on the left side.

4.0 Turn RIGHT at trail intersection on the left side. Head toward Kelly Lake.

4.3 Continue STRAIGHT at trail junction on the left side (Cross Canyon Trail West.)

5.0 Continue STRAIGHT at single-track trail intersection on the right side.

5.9 Continue STRAIGHT at Jackson Trail Junction on the right side. Be sure to enjoy the expansive views from the ridge line off both sides of the trail.

7.2 Follow along stream after long descent.

7.5 Cross stream.

7.7 Turn RIGHT to get to Kelly Lake. Continue to far side of lake and then return back the way you came.

12.1 Turn LEFT at trail intersection to return toward Gilroy Hot Springs.

16.1 End of the ride at the trailhead on Gilroy Hot Springs Road.

Further Information

Henry Coe State Park: (408) 779-2728

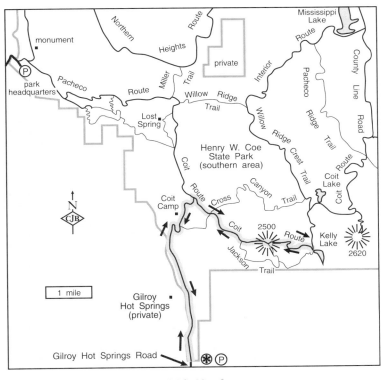

Ride No. 6

Kelly Lake.

7

Campbell
Los Gatos Creek Trail

Region: *South Bay*
Difficulty Rating: *Easy*
Skill Level: *Beginner*
Elevation Gain: *300 feet*

Total Distance: *17 miles*
Off-Road Distance: *14 miles*
Riding Time: *2 hours*
Total Calories: *600*

About the Ride

The Los Gatos Creek Trail is a very popular multi-use trail in the South Bay. Weekends find the trail filled with walkers, runners, in-line skaters, and cyclists. It almost goes without saying that the cyclist should be very wary of the others and speeds should be kept reasonable.

Following Los Gatos Creek, the trail has been expanded regularly and promises to go all the way to San Jose in the near future. This out-and-back ride starts in Campbell and follows the trail to Los Gatos via picturesque Vasona Park. When you pass through Vasona Park, be sure to take a close look at the Billy Jones Wildcat Railroad, a narrow gauge railroad intended primarily for the entertainment of children and their parents. Surface roads take you from Vasona Park to central Los Gatos. Past Old Town Los Gatos, you will again pick up the trail, a dirt path leading to Lexington Dam. The top of the dam is the turn-around point.

While the trail is basically flat, the final section leading up to the dam is quite steep and most people need to walk their bikes.

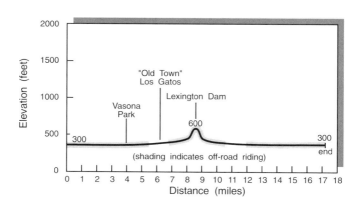

Starting Point

Start the ride at the Pruneyard Shopping Center in Campbell. To get there, take Highway 17 south and get off at Hamilton Avenue. Turn left on Hamilton Avenue and then right onto Bascom Avenue. The Pruneyard is located on the right side at the corner of Campbell Avenue. Park in the rear of the shopping center where there is an access gate to the Los Gatos Creek Trail.

Mile Markers

0.0   The bike path access is located at the north end of the parking lot in the rear of the Pruneyard Center. Get on the path and proceed SOUTH toward Los Gatos.

1.4   Follow the bike path over the bridge to get on the west side of the creek.

3.3   Get off the trail at its end and turn LEFT onto Lark Avenue, cross the bridge and get back on the bike path.

3.8   Vasona Park dam on the right side. Continue around the lake.

4.9   At the trestle for the Billy Jones Wildcat Railroad, do not cross the bridge, but instead, cross the tracks and continue on the dirt section of the trail.

5.3   Trail ends. Turn RIGHT onto Roberts Road.

5.5   Turn LEFT on University Avenue.

6.3   "Old Town" Los Gatos is on the left side.

6.5   Turn LEFT on East Main Street.

6.8   Cross overpass for highway 17 and then turn RIGHT onto the continuation of Los Gatos Creek Trail.

8.6   Top of the dam at Lexington Reservoir. Return back the way you came.

10.4   Turn LEFT onto East Main Street.

10.7   Turn RIGHT onto University Avenue.

11.7   Turn RIGHT onto Roberts Road.

11.9   Turn LEFT to get on Los Gatos Creek Trail into Vasona Park.

17.2   End of the ride back at the Pruneyard Center.

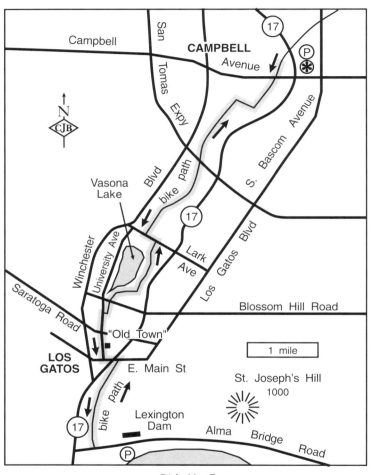

Ride No. 7

Bay Area Mountain Bike Trails

8 Aptos
The Loma Prieta Earthquake Epicenter

Region: *South Bay*	**Total Distance:** *9 miles*
Difficulty Rating: *Easy*	**Off-Road Distance:** *3 miles*
Skill Level: *Beginner*	**Riding Time:** *1-2 hours*
Elevation Gain: *120 feet*	**Total Calories:** *200*

About the Ride

When the Loma Prieta Earthquake shook the Bay Area in October of 1989, extensive damage resulted in the Santa Cruz Mountains and elsewhere. The epicenter of the temblor was determined to have been inside the boundary of The Forest of Nisene Marks State Park in Aptos, a mile or more below the surface. This ride follows an easy out-and-back route to the marker designating the approximate site of the epicenter.

Starting at the inconspicuous and in fact, somewhat hard-to-find entrance to the park, the route follows along Aptos Creek Road to the park entrance and then continues along Aptos Creek Fire Road within the park. The remains of the old logging mill and other points of interest lie along the route to the epicenter. Fabulous hiking trails through lush ferns and redwoods abound within the park. Bikes, however, are restricted to the fire roads. Be sure to stay on designated trails at all times.

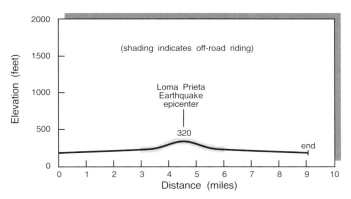

Starting Point

To get to the starting point, take Highway 1 south from Santa Cruz. Get off in Aptos at the Seacliff Beach-Aptos exit and turn left onto State Park Drive. Turn right onto Soquel Drive and follow it under the railroad bridge, after which you will find Aptos Creek Road on the left side. Park near this intersection to begin the ride.

Mile Markers

- 0.0 Proceed NORTH into the park on Aptos Creek Road.
- 1.8 Picnic area on the right side.
- 1.9 Cross bridge.
- 2.9 Porter Family Picnic Area — gate to the Aptos Creek Fire Road is on the left side.
- 3.2 Cross Aptos Creek.
- 3.5 Loma Prieta Mill site on the left side.
- 4.4 Cross bridge over the creek.
- 4.5 Loma Prieta Earthquake epicenter marker on the right side. Return out the way you came in.
- 9.0 End of the ride at Soquel Drive.

Further Information

Forest of Nisene Marks State Park: (408) 335-4598

Epicenter of the Loma Prieta Earthquake.

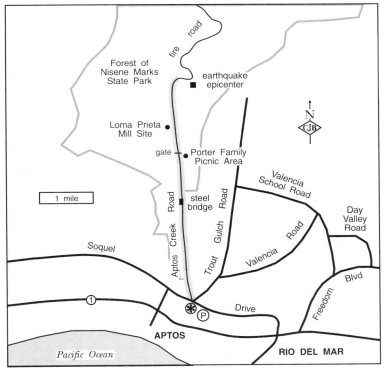

Forest of
Nisene Marks
State Park

fire road

earthquake
epicenter

Loma Prieta
Mill Site

gate

Porter Family
Picnic Area

1 mile

Aptos Creek Road

steel
bridge

Trout Gulch Road

Valencia
School Road

Day
Valley
Road

Valencia Road

Soquel

Freedom Blvd

Drive

APTOS

Pacific Ocean

RIO DEL MAR

N
CJB

Ride No. 8

9 Aptos

The Forest of Nisene Marks and Sand Point Overlook

Region: *South Bay*
Difficulty Rating: *Moderate*
Skill Level: *Intermediate*
Elevation Gain: *1500 feet*

Total Distance: *22 miles*
Off-Road Distance: *10 miles*
Riding Time: *4 hours*
Total Calories: *800*

About the Ride

The Forest of Nisene Marks State Park is located on property once owned by the Loma Prieta Lumber Company and was logged extensively in the early part of the twentieth century. In the 1950s, the Marks family purchased the property and halted logging operations to save the redwoods. In 1963, the property was given to the State of California by the Marks children in memory of their mother, Nisene, with the stipulation that the park be operated as a semi-wilderness, without major improvements. As a result, there are no visitor centers or ranger stations, and facilities are somewhat spare.

This ride will take you into the park along a wide fire road. You will pass the Loma Prieta Earthquake epicenter and then climb rather steeply toward the Sand Point Overlook, a great place to rest and to savor the views of the coast off the hillside to the west. This is the highest spot on the ride as the route then leads down and out of the park onto Olive Springs Road, making several stream crossings along the way. From there, Soquel-San Jose Road will take you to central Soquel and Soquel Drive, back to Aptos and the start point.

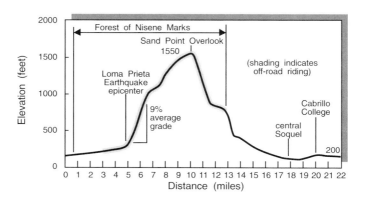

Starting Point

To get to the starting point, take Highway 1 south from Santa Cruz. Get off in Aptos at the Seacliff Beach-Aptos exit and turn left onto State Park Drive. Turn right onto Soquel Drive and follow it under the railroad bridge, after which you will find Aptos Creek Road on the left side. Park near this intersection to begin the ride.

Mile Markers

0.0 Proceed NORTH into the park on Aptos Creek Road.

1.8 Picnic area on the right side.

1.9 Cross bridge.

2.9 Porter Family Picnic Area — gate to the Aptos Creek Fire Road is on the left side.

3.2 Cross Aptos Creek.

3.5 Loma Prieta Mill site on the left side.

4.4 Cross bridge over the creek.

4.5 Loma Prieta Earthquake epicenter marker on the right side. Continue past.

4.6 Begin to climb steeply.

9.0 Sand Point Overlook on left side. Turn LEFT onto West Ridge Trail toward Olive Springs Road.

9.5 West Ridge Trail Camp on the right side.

10.4 Gate.

10.6 Bear RIGHT at the trail split. Trail gets more narrow.

11.0 Turn RIGHT onto fire road.

11.9 Stream crossings.

12.2 Last stream crossing — climb steeply for a short distance.

12.3 Gate — turn LEFT onto Olive Springs Road.

13.6 Turn LEFT onto Soquel-San Jose Road.

14.7 Country store on the right side.

18.1 Turn LEFT onto Soquel Drive in central Soquel.

19.8 Cabrillo College.

22.1 End of the ride at Aptos Creek Road intersection.

Further Information

Forest of Nisene Marks State Park: (408) 335-4598

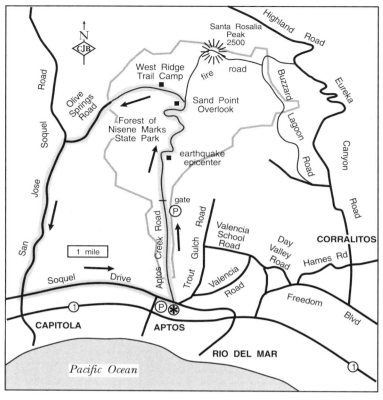

Ride No. 9

Looking toward the coast from Sand Point Overlook.

10   Aptos
The Forest of Nisene Marks —
Corralitos Loop

Region: *South Bay*
Difficulty Rating: *Difficult*
Skill Level: *Intermediate*
Elevation Gain: *2500 feet*

Total Distance: *33 miles*
Off-Road Distance: *13 miles*
Riding Time: *5 hours*
Total Calories: *1200*

About the Ride

The Forest of Nisene Marks State Park is the home to giant redwoods, the ones that survived the extensive logging operations of former times. Numerous hiking trails meander through the heavy moss-covered forest along shady creeks and past lush ferns. While the single-track hiking trails are off limits to cyclists, the fire roads offer some of the finest mountain biking in the South Bay. During the hot summer months, the cool coastal climate can be an especially refreshing relief. Just east of the park lie the apple orchards and strawberry fields of Corralitos.

This ride samples all the local environs, as it leads first along the rolling terrain of the quiet country roads to Corralitos and to its legendary sausage store. From Corralitos, Eureka Canyon Road winds its way uphill, first along a gentle grade and then getting somewhat steeper. At the top lies the rear entrance to The Forest of Nisene Marks State Park. More climbing along the fire road within the park will take you over Santa Rosalia Peak (about 2,500-foot elevation) and then it's all downhill through the redwoods. Sand Point Overlook, about halfway down, offers spectacular views of the coast. At the bottom, the Loma Prieta Earthquake epicenter invites you make your own pilgrimage down the side trail to the focal point of the great earthquake of 1989.

The climb up Eureka Canyon Road is a big one, but the grade is fairly modest (compared to most fire roads) and the scenery is best enjoyed when you go slow anyway. The route through the park follows wide fire roads which don't require any advanced skills to negotiate.

Starting Point

To get to the starting point, take Highway 1 south from Santa Cruz. Get off in Aptos at the Seacliff Beach-Aptos exit and turn left onto State Park Drive. Turn right onto Soquel Drive and follow it under the railroad bridge, after which you will find Aptos Creek Road on the left side. Park near this intersection to begin the ride.

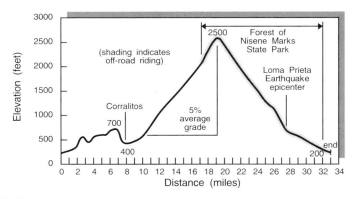

Mile Markers

0.0 Proceed EAST on Soquel Drive.

0.1 Turn LEFT onto Trout Gulch Road.

0.6 Turn RIGHT onto Valencia Road.

3.3 Turn RIGHT onto Day Valley Road.

5.3 Turn LEFT onto Freedom Boulevard.

5.4 Turn LEFT onto Hames Road.

7.6 Turn LEFT onto Eureka Canyon Road.

17.1 Turn LEFT onto Buzzard Lagoon Road (dirt road).

17.8 Turn RIGHT at trail split onto Aptos Creek Fire Road.

18.8 Gate into Forest of Nisene Marks State Park.

19.0 High point — 2,500-foot elevation.

19.7 Soquel Demonstration Forest on right side.

23.1 Continue STRAIGHT at Sand Point Overlook.

27.6 Loma Prieta Earthquake epicenter marker on left side.

33.0 End of the ride at Soquel Drive.

Further Information

Forest of Nisene Marks State Park: (408) 335-4598

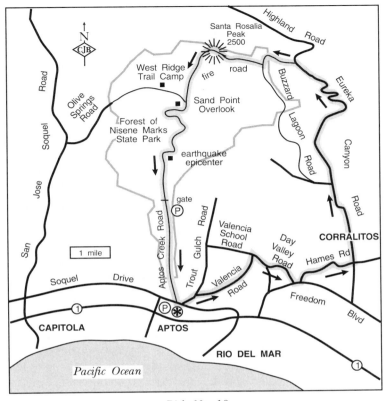

Ride No. 10

Along Aptos Creek Fire Road.

11 Soquel

Soquel Demonstration Forest

Region: *South Bay*
Difficulty Rating: *Difficult*
Skill Level: *Advanced*
Elevation Gain: *1900 feet*

Total Distance: *13 miles*
Off-Road Distance: *11 miles*
Riding Time: *2-3 hours*
Total Calories: *1100*

About the Ride

The California Department of Forestry operates "demonstration forests" throughout the State to show how to manage timber resources in ways that respect the natural aspects of the forests. At the same time, the management methods provide for sensible harvesting of lumber and for recreation by the general public. The Soquel Demonstration Forest, located adjacent to The Forest of Nisene Marks State Park, is one recent addition to the system, having been added in 1990.

This ride follows trails through the forest which are particularly unique. While most state and county parks and open space preserves forbid bikes from using single-track trails, the Soquel Demonstration Forest does not. Needless to say, rules often change, and when you do this ride, be sure to check the information boards within the park to confirm that this situation is still the case. Avoid unmarked trails, as they may lead to private property. The legal trails throughout the forest are well marked and easy to follow.

The route starts at the entrance to the park located on Highland Way in the heart of the Santa Cruz Mountains. It initially follows the paved road away from the park entrance and up the hill toward the rear entrance of The Forest of Nisene Marks State Park. The dirt road into Nisene Marks leads uphill some more before it reaches the entrance to Soquel Demonstration Forest. From here, single-track trails offer all the challenge you could ask for. Narrow, winding, sometimes steep, and often overgrown, the trails lead through the heavy forest to an overlook point with sensational views to the west. Steep downhill sections may require you to lower your seat to avoid the dreaded "over-the-handlebar-dismount." At the bottom of the hill, the wide Hihn's Mill Fire Road will take you out of the forest along a steady uphill grade.

Starting Point

To get to the starting point, take Highway 17 south from Los Gatos toward Santa Cruz. At the top of the mountains, get off at Summit Road and follow it back over the freeway. Continue on Summit Road for about 4 miles and then continue another 5.5 miles as Summit Road changes to Highland Way. The trailhead is on the right side of the road and is easy to miss, so look closely for it. Parking is permitted along the road and more parking is available off the road about a ¼-mile in.

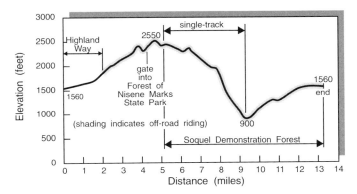

Mile Markers

0.0 Proceed SOUTH on Highland Way.

0.6 Camp Loma.

2.0 Turn RIGHT onto Buzzard Lagoon Road. This is a dirt road which leads into The Forest of Nisene Marks State Park.

2.4 Gate on right side — private property — do not enter.

2.5 Continue STRAIGHT through gate.

2.9 Turn RIGHT onto unmarked Aptos Creek Fire Road (Buzzard Lagoon Road continues straight ahead.)

3.5 First of several unmarked trails on right side — do not enter.

4.3 Continue STRAIGHT past gate into the Forest of Nisene Marks State Park.

5.2 Turn RIGHT off the fire road to enter Soquel Demonstration Forest State Park on Ridge Trail. Look for the information board and clear trail markings. Prepare to ride on narrow single-track trails with heavy growth and down steep sections with lots of bumps.

5.9 Bear LEFT to stay on Ridge Trail — Corral Trail goes to the right.

6.8 Turn LEFT to stay on Ridge Trail — Sulphur Springs Trail continues straight ahead. Take Sulphur Springs Trail if you wish to avoid the remaining single-track trails (they are very steep in places.)

7.4 Overlook on the left side — great views to the coast.

7.8 Turn RIGHT onto Tractor Trail — Ridge Trail continues straight ahead, but has no outlet. Prepare for steep descent.

9.3 Turn RIGHT onto Hihn's Mill Road, a wide fire road.

10.6 Continue STRAIGHT at intersection with Sulphur Springs Trail on the right side.

13.0 Continue STRAIGHT past the gate to exit the demonstration forest.

13.2 End of the ride at Highland Way trail head.

Further Information

Soquel Demonstration State Forest: (408) 475-8643

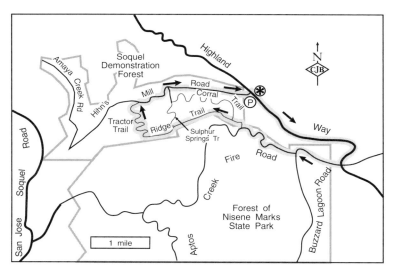

Ride No. 11

12 Santa Cruz
Henry Cowell Redwoods State Park

Region: *South Bay*
Difficulty Rating: *Easy*
Skill Level: *Intermediate*
Elevation Gain: *700 feet*

Total Distance: *8 miles*
Off-Road Distance: *5 miles*
Riding Time: *2 hours*
Total Calories: *400*

About the Ride

The Roaring Camp and Big Trees Railroad have served for years as fine family entertainment in the town of Felton, located near Santa Cruz. With its fully-operational steam train carrying people of all ages through the redwood forests along the old logging route, Roaring Camp has, to some extent, preserved the magic of the old days. Hikers and cyclists in the nearby Henry Cowell Redwoods State Park can often hear the sound of the locomotive reverberating through the forest as it releases the pressures of its expanding steam.

While this ride through Henry Cowell Park is rated as an easy one, there is one sizable hill that cannot be taken for granted. Nevertheless, the ride is short and on the whole, quite flat.

The ride begins in the center of tiny Felton. The route will take you south on Highway 9 a short distance to the park entrance. Just within the park is a visitor center which has information about the park and the surrounding redwood forests. Near the visitor center is a scenic walking path leading through some of the most dramatic of the remaining redwood trees. Back on your bike, you will then follow a paved service road through nearly the entire length of the park and then climb a relatively small hill along a narrow park trail. At the top is an observation deck with views of the surrounding forest. The return back is along the same way you went in.

Starting Point

Begin the ride in the center of Felton. To get there, take Highway 17 south toward Santa Cruz and get off at the Mount Herman Road exit. Follow Mount Herman Road to where it ends at Graham Hill Road. Turn right to enter Felton and park anywhere around town.

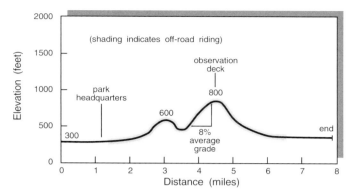

Mile Markers

0.0 Proceed SOUTH on Highway 9 away from Felton.

0.6 Turn LEFT into Henry Cowell Redwoods State Park entrance.

1.2 Park headquarters.

1.4 Restrooms and concession area. Look for a road at the back of the restrooms, this is Pipeline Road. Get on the road and head south, away from the concessions.

2.0 Cross under the railroad tracks.

2.5 Intersection with Rincon Trail on the right side.

3.7 Turn LEFT onto Powder Mill Trail.

4.3 Turn LEFT onto Ridge Trail and head toward the observation deck.

4.5 Observation deck is on the right side. Trail continues straight ahead.

5.0 Turn RIGHT onto Pipeline Road and return to concession area.

6.5 Turn LEFT at parking lot to get back on the road to exit the park.

7.3 Turn RIGHT onto Highway 9.

7.9 End of the ride back in Felton.

Further Information

Cowell Redwoods State Park: (408) 335-4598

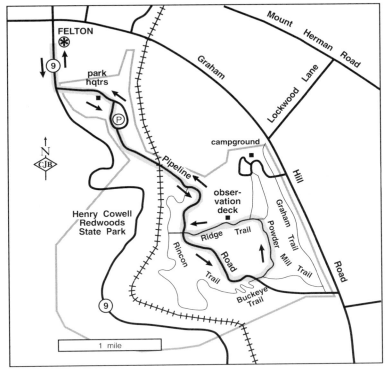

Ride No. 12

13   Saratoga

Big Basin State Park

Region: *South Bay*
Difficulty Rating: *Moderate*
Skill Level: *Beginner*
Elevation Gain: *1500 feet*

Total Distance: *16 miles*
Off-Road Distance: *11 miles*
Riding Time: *2-3 hours*
Total Calories: *700*

About the Ride

Big Basin Redwoods State Park is home to some of the most majestic redwoods in the State and has long been enjoyed by South Bay Area residents for its extensive hiking, camping, and picnicking. Logged heavily in its early years, Big Basin became a state park in 1902. You can still see the stumps of many of the original redwoods surrounded by second growth trees, which are rapidly reclaiming the forest.

This ride takes you around the eastern end of the park, the area most easily accessible. It starts at a point about 3 miles from park headquarters and begins by climbing along North China Grade Road, a paved road, to get to a back entrance into Big Basin. Middle Ridge Fire Trail takes you into the park to an overlook along Hihn Hammond Fire Road. From this point you can get a clear look at the Waddell Creek Basin extending all the way to the sea. The return route passes park headquarters. Be sure to explore the Nature Lodge and take the short hike along the Redwood Trail Loop. Back on your bike, finish the ride by continuing along the paved road through the park and then along the road again to get back to your starting point.

Most of the ride is along wide fire trails and paved service roads. Some riding on the main road is necessary, so it is important to be careful and to ride in single file.

Starting Point

Big Basin is located in the Santa Cruz Mountains below Saratoga. To get there, take Big Basin Way (Highway 9) out of Saratoga. Big Basin Way becomes Congress Springs Road just out of town and climbs to Skyline Boulevard at the top. Continue across Skyline Boulevard for about 6 miles and then turn right onto Highway 236 toward Big Basin. The intersection with China Grade is located about 5 miles down Highway 236. Park near this corner to start the ride.

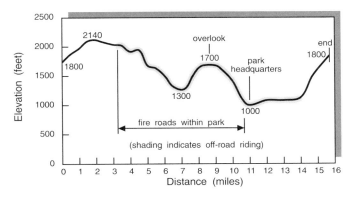

Mile Markers

0.0 Begin the ride by going up the hill on North China Grade Road.

2.4 Continue STRAIGHT at the road intersection on the right side.

3.3 Turn LEFT into Big Basin onto Middle Ridge Fire Road.

4.1 Turn LEFT to stay on Middle Ridge Fire Road.

4.2 Continue past the gate.

6.2 Continue STRAIGHT to stay on Middle Ridge Fire Road.

6.6 Turn RIGHT onto Gazos Creek Road and then immediately turn LEFT to get back on Middle Ridge Fire Road.

7.4 Turn RIGHT onto Hihn Hammond Road to head toward the overlook.

8.6 Overlook on the left side — great views of entire Waddell Creek basin. Return back on Hihn Hammond Road.

9.8 Continue STRAIGHT at the intersection with Middle Ridge Fire Road on the left side.

10.3 Turn LEFT onto paved path (continuation of Hihn Hammond Road.)

10.6 Continue past the gate and turn LEFT at the path split.

11.0 Park headquarters on the right side. Turn LEFT to go back into the park and proceed on the paved road.

11.3 Continue STRAIGHT at the road intersection on the left side.

12.2 Continue past gate — road turns into a paved path.

12.4 Cross bridge.

13.5 Cross another bridge and begin climbing.

14.6 End of path at gate — turn LEFT onto Highway 236.

15.7 End of the ride.

Further Information

Big Basin State Park: (408) 338-6132

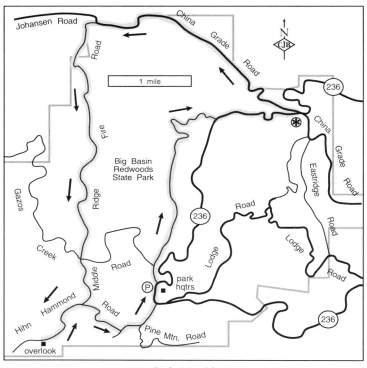

Ride No. 13

14 Santa Cruz
Wilder Ranch
State Historic Preserve

Region: *South Bay*
Difficulty Rating: *Moderate*
Skill Level: *Intermediate*
Elevation Gain: *1600 feet*

Total Distance: *18 miles*
Off-Road Distance: *16 miles*
Riding Time: *3 hours*
Total Calories: *1100*

About the Ride

Single-track trails through forests and meadows, numerous stream crossings, and a spectacular ride along the cliffs at the edge of the ocean give Wilder Ranch a variety rarely found in mountain biking. Formerly an operating ranch, it is now a cultural preserve, only recently being opened to the public.

This ride is conveniently divided into three distinct loops, each emanating from very near the park headquarters. In this way, the ride can be tailored to suit any particular need. The first loop, 3 miles in length, is the easiest. Totally flat, it takes you out away from the park headquarters and follows Old Cove Landing Trail along the edge of the shoreline before returning back to the starting point. You definitely do not want to miss this section.

The second loop takes you through the ranch compound, where you can explore the old buildings. It then heads inland and uphill along a wide fire trail before returning along a narrow and challenging single-track.

The third and final loop is the longest. It leads along ridges and then through meadows, finally passing through a eucalyptus grove at its highest point. The return has several stream crossings and then passes through a heavy forest before coming out on the main road, Highway 1. The return to park headquarters is along busy Highway 1, but a wide shoulder makes it a safe ride.

Starting Point

Wilder Ranch is located on Highway 1, about 2 miles north of Santa Cruz. There is a modest day use fee for cars that can be avoided by parking on the main road and riding in.

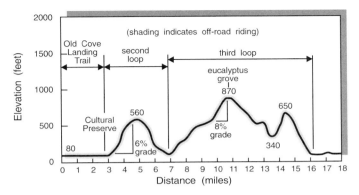

Mile Markers

0.0 Proceed out of parking lot onto Old Cove Landing Trail.

2.1 Continue STRAIGHT toward park headquarters where trail becomes dirt road.

2.5 Back at parking area where this loop began. Proceed down paved path toward Cultural Preserve.

2.6 Turn LEFT into ranch compound. Continue on the trail around the LEFT side of the stables and through the tunnel.

3.1 Continue STRAIGHT at the trail intersection on the left side, then continue STRAIGHT at the main trail intersection to get on Engelsman Trail.

3.6 Bear RIGHT to stay on trail.

4.8 Continue STRAIGHT at major trail intersection on the left and begin Lime Kiln Trail.

5.3 Begin single-track section (Wagonwheel Trail) and start to descend steeply.

6.9 Turn RIGHT sharply onto wide trail.

7.0 Bear RIGHT and begin to climb on Vaca Trail.

7.7 Single-track trail intersection on the left side.

8.4 Bear RIGHT onto single-track Twin Oaks Trail.

9.2 Bear RIGHT at trail split to get onto Bobcat Trail, continue through the woods, across a stream and then turn LEFT onto Venado Trail.

9.6 Turn RIGHT sharply at 4-way trail intersection onto Charcoal Trail.

10.8 Pass through eucalyptus grove.

12.8 Continue STRAIGHT at trail intersection on the left (Bobcat Trail). Proceed through the same meadow previously encountered (Venado Trail).

13.0 Back at the major trail intersection, turn LEFT and then turn RIGHT onto first single-track trail (Enchanted Loop Trail).

13.8 Continue STRAIGHT at trail intersection on right.

14.4 Turn RIGHT sharply onto Sea Ridge Trail toward Highway 1.

15.9 Turn LEFT onto Highway 1.

17.8 Turn RIGHT into Wilder Ranch State Park entrance.

18.0 End of the ride at the parking lot.

Further Information

Wilder Ranch State Park: (408) 423-9703

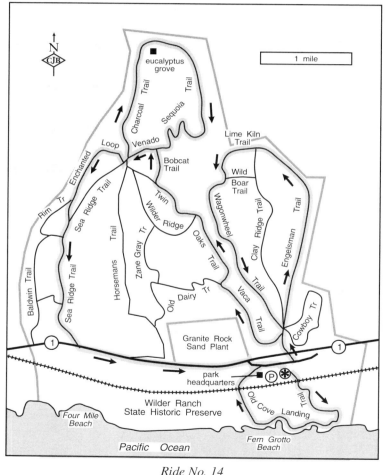

Ride No. 14

The Pacific coastline in Wilder Ranch State Park.

The San Francisco Peninsula

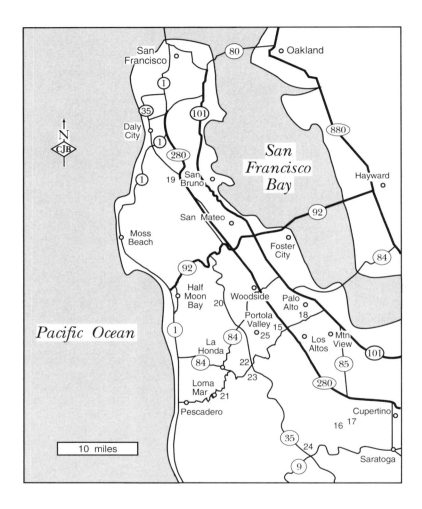

15 Palo Alto
The Arastradero Preserve

Region: *Peninsula*
Difficulty Rating: *Easy*
Skill Level: *Beginner*
Elevation Gain: *500 feet*

Total Distance: *5 miles*
Off-Road Distance: *4 miles*
Riding Time: *1-2 hours*
Total Calories: *500*

About the Ride

The Arastradero Preserve is administered by the Midpeninsula Open Space District and consists mainly of rolling pasture land and grassy fields. Along Arastradero Creek and around the lake, trees provide welcome shade on hot summer days.

Its close proximity to Palo Alto and other Bay Area population centers makes Arastradero Preserve a popular place for hikers, runners, cyclists, and equestrians. Keep in mind that, if you decide to explore the preserve on your own, be aware that some trails do not permit bikes and consequently must be avoided. Trails are not always well-marked, so be careful to follow the directions closely.

This easy tour is a sweet and simple introduction to mountain biking. Some small hills and narrow single-track trails allow the beginner cyclist to develop riding skills without the necessity of tackling monstrous hill climbs. The route takes you from the main parking lot into the preserve along various trails which wind around and about and up and down in what might be thought of as a rather haphazard path. The idea is to get a flavor of the entire park by visiting each of its sections. After exiting at the opposite end, the return along Arastradero Road is quite scenic and ends with an exhilarating downhill.

Starting Point

The ride starts at the parking lot for Arastradero Preserve. To get there take Highway 280 to Palo Alto and get off at Page Mill Road. Head west on Page Mill for about ¼-mile and then turn right onto Arastradero Road. The parking lot is located about ½-mile down Arastradero Road.

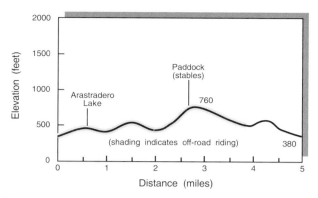

Mile Markers

0.0 From the parking lot, turn LEFT onto Arastradero Road, heading toward Page Mill Road.

0.2 Turn RIGHT to enter the preserve. Carry your bike across the barrier.

0.4 Bear RIGHT to stay on the main trail at the junction with a trail on the left. Just after this, bear LEFT at another trail split.

0.6 Arastradero Lake on the left side.

0.7 Turn LEFT just past the lake to get on Corte Madera Trail.

1.0 Turn RIGHT onto unmarked Acorn Trail and climb a short hill.

1.2 Continue STRAIGHT at the top of the hill at the main trail intersection (Meadowlark Trail) and continue on Acorn Trail.

1.5 Turn RIGHT at the end of Acorn Trail and go around the chain link gate to get on the gravel service road.

1.8 Turn RIGHT at the point where there is a preserve exit gate on the left side.

2.0 Turn RIGHT onto unmarked Meadowlark Trail.

2.3 Continue STRAIGHT at the intersection with Acorn Trail. This is the same intersection you passed through previously along Acorn Trail.

2.7 Paddock on the right side.

2.8 Continue past the gate.

3.3 Carry your bike across the barrier and continue on the paved road.

3.7 Turn RIGHT onto Arastradero Road.

5.0 End of the ride back at the parking area.

Further Information

Midpeninsula Regional Open Space District: (415) 949-5500

Bay Area Mountain Bike Trails

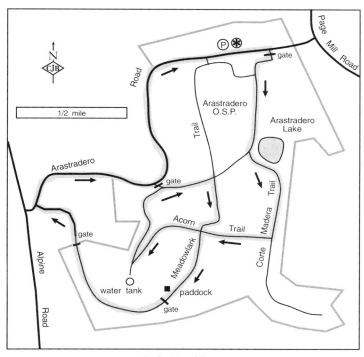

Ride No. 15

Meadowlark Trail in Arastradero Preserve.

16 Cupertino

Monte Bello Open Space Preserve

Region: *Peninsula*
Difficulty Rating: *Difficult*
Skill Level: *Intermediate*
Elevation Gain: *2500 feet*

Total Distance: *17 miles*
Off-Road Distance: *7 miles*
Riding Time: *3-4 hours*
Total Calories: *1400*

About the Ride

The upper Stevens Creek watershed, from the grassy slopes of Monte Bello Ridge to the brush and oak-covered woodlands below, comprises the Monte Bello Open Space Preserve. Located in the Santa Cruz Mountains high above Palo Alto, Monte Bello is the largest area managed by the Midpeninsula Open Space District.

While the primary access points for Monte Bello are along Page Mill Road about one mile from Skyline Boulevard near the top of the mountain range, there are less-known ways to get in, as well. This ride uses one of those and starts well below Monte Bello at Stevens Creek Reservoir near the town of Cupertino. The route follows along rural country roads as it takes you around the reservoir and into the lush Stevens Canyon, following along Stevens Creek toward its source high in the hills. At the end of Stevens Canyon Road is a "back door" into Monte Bello, an unobtrusive gate connecting to Canyon Trail.

Canyon trail climbs steadily at first through dense growth and then along the ridge as the fauna thins out. Indian Creek Trail and Black Mountain Trail climb steeply toward Black Mountain (2,780-foot elevation) where there are superb views of the watershed to the west and of the entire Santa Clara Valley, to the east. A side trip along Waterwheel Trail leads to the exit gate onto Monte Bello Road and a speedy descent along Montebello Road back to the starting point.

Steep uphill sections of the ride along Indian Creek Trail and narrow sections along Canyon Trail provide plenty of challenge. Be sure to carry adequate water as there are no services along the route.

Starting Point

The ride starts in Cupertino on Stevens Canyon Road, just past Stevens Creek Dam. Take Highway 280 and get off at the Foothill Expressway and Grant Road exit. Note that there are several exits for Foothill Expressway, so be sure to take the one in Cupertino. Head west on Foothill Boulevard and cross Stevens Creek Boulevard. Continue straight as the road changes name to Stevens Canyon Road. Continue past the dam. Just after the intersection with Montebello Road on the right you will find a small park. Start the ride there.

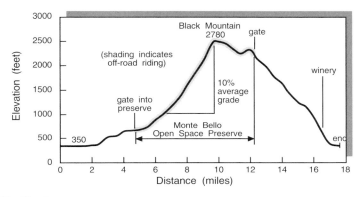

Mile Markers

0.0 Proceed WEST on Stevens Canyon Road, away from the dam and toward the mountains.

1.2 Bear RIGHT to stay on Stevens Canyon Road.

2.9 Redwood Gulch Road intersection on the left side.

4.8 Continue STRAIGHT past the gate at the end of the road (Canyon Trail).

5.7 Very narrow section of trail.

6.1 Bear RIGHT at the trail intersection on the left.

6.4 Continue STRAIGHT at trail intersection to stay on Canyon Trail (Grizzly Flat Trail is on the left).

8.4 Bear RIGHT onto Indian Creek Trail, heading steeply up toward Black Mountain.

8.9 Continue STRAIGHT at trail intersection on the left.

9.1 Another trail intersection on the left.

9.3 Third trail intersection on the left.

9.4 Black Mountain summit at the microwave towers — 2,780 feet.

10.3 Turn RIGHT onto Waterwheel Trail.

11.7 Continue past the barrier at the end of the trail and turn RIGHT onto Montebello Road.

16.8 Turn RIGHT onto Stevens Canyon Road.

16.9 End of the ride at the parking area.

Further Information

Midpeninsula Regional Open Space District: (415) 949-5500

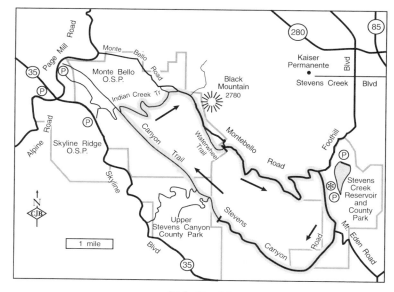

Ride No. 16

Waterwheel Trail in Monte Bello.

17 Cupertino
Fremont Older Open Space Preserve

Region: *Peninsula*
Difficulty Rating: *Moderate*
Skill Level: *Intermediate*
Elevation Gain: *1300 feet*

Total Distance: *8 miles*
Off-Road Distance: *8 miles*
Riding Time: *1-2 hours*
Total Calories: *700*

About the Ride

Fremont Older Open Space Preserve, while small in size, has the advantage of being close to the population centers of the Peninsula. As a result, it is an ideal place for a fast after-work ride. It is both easy to get to and quick to tour. In spite of this, there is still some substantial challenge to be had there. Steep grades and narrow single-track offer advanced mountain bikers plenty of excitement. Beginners can take their time and walk their bikes when the grades get too difficult to handle.

The route actually starts within Stevens Creek County Park. A short ride along a flat trail leading from the parking lot will quickly take you into Fremont Older, which is directly adjacent. Once inside Fremont Older, a steep climb along a wide fire road leads to a ridge overlooking the canyon. Rolling terrain along the ridge top leads to the return along a narrow trail with expansive views of the Santa Clara Valley. A side trip around Seven Springs Loop will take you down a steep decline and then back up to the ridge along a single-track trail with tight switchbacks. The return off the ridge top down to the parking lot follows the fire road that brought you up.

The trails are well-marked and are often heavily used by hikers and equestrians (there is a popular stable on the border of the preserve). Always be courteous and yield the trail to all others whenever necessary.

Starting Point

Start the ride in the main parking lot at Stevens Creek County Park, just below the dam. Take Highway 280 to Cupertino and get off at the Foothill Expressway and Grant Road exit. Note that there are several exits for Foothill Expressway, so be sure to take the one in Cupertino. Head west on Foothill Boulevard and cross Stevens Creek Boulevard. Continue straight as the road changes name to Stevens Canyon Road. Look for the park entrance on the left. Go down the hill and park in the lot to begin the ride.

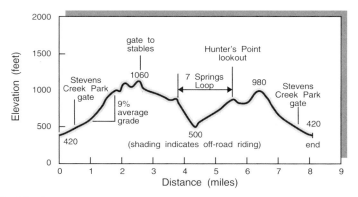

Mile Markers

0.0 Proceed away from the parking lot on the paved road into the park.

0.2 Turn LEFT onto Old Canyon Trail, heading toward Fremont Older.

0.5 Continue past the gate into Fremont Older Preserve and begin climbing.

1.3 Trail intersection on the left side.

1.8 Continue STRAIGHT at the trail intersection on the left side.

1.9 Bear RIGHT at trail split and continue climbing.

2.1 Continue STRAIGHT at major trail junction (Lookout Trail goes to the right.)

2.3 Continue STRAIGHT at trail junction on right side.

2.5 Make a sharp LEFT turn toward Hunter's Point and Prospect Road just before the gate into the stables.

2.6 Bear LEFT at trail split to stay on main trail.

3.0 Bear RIGHT at trail split to head toward Hunter's Point.

3.3 Turn RIGHT onto main fire road.

3.6 Bear LEFT to stay on fire road (Prospect Road is to the right.)

3.7 Continue STRAIGHT at trail intersection on the left.

3.8 Bear RIGHT toward 7 Springs Loop. Stay on main fire road and begin to descend steeply.

4.3 At park boundary, turn LEFT onto single-track and begin to climb back up.

5.1 Continue STRAIGHT on single-track at main trail junction.

5.3 Turn RIGHT sharply back at main trail junction and head uphill toward Hunter's Point Lookout.

5.4 Hunter's Point Lookout — great views. Return back down.

5.5 Turn RIGHT onto main fire road toward Stevens Creek Park.

5.6 Continue STRAIGHT at trail intersection on right.

5.7 Bear RIGHT at trail split toward Stevens Creek Park.

6.1 Continue STRAIGHT on main fire road at single-track intersection on the left.

6.3 Turn RIGHT onto the main fire road.

7.5 Gate into Stevens Creek Park.

7.9 Turn RIGHT onto paved road.

8.1 End of the ride at the parking lot.

Further Information

Midpeninsula Regional Open Space District: (415) 949-5500

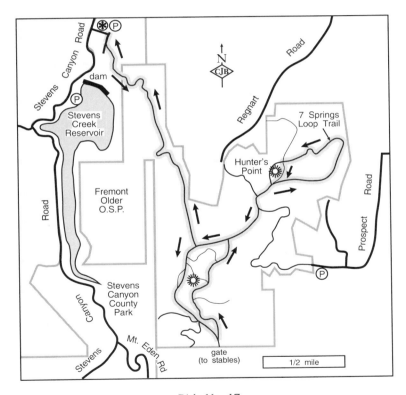

Ride No. 17

18 Mountain View

Mountain View Shoreline Park

Region: *Peninsula*
Difficulty Rating: *Easy*
Skill Level: *Beginner*
Elevation Gain: *40 feet*

Total Distance: *20 miles*
Off-Road Distance: *7 miles*
Riding Time: *3 hours*
Total Calories: *400*

About the Ride

Beginner mountain bike enthusiasts will love this ride. Completely flat except for a couple of freeway overpasses, it follows a route that includes Stanford University, fashionable residential areas of bicycle-friendly Palo Alto, and Mountain View's scenic Shoreline Park. While riding along surface roads is a requirement, the wide bike lanes, provided by the forward-thinking City of Palo Alto, make the ride quite safe. Car interference is minimal.

Shoreline Park includes a public golf course, sailing and windsurfing lake, and Shoreline Amphitheater. Trails through the park offer rare glimpses of nesting and migrating birds, as well as stunning views of San Francisco Bay. Walkers, runners, and cyclists share the trails within the park, so be careful and be especially courteous to others at all times.

Just north of Shoreline Park lies the Palo Alto Baylands Preserve with trails leading around the periphery of Palo Alto Municipal Airport.

The ride starts at the football stadium on the campus of Stanford University, where there is plenty of parking except on game days. From there, the route will take you on a leisurely tour through some of Palo Alto's nicest neighborhoods, past tasteful homes with meticulously manicured landscaping and quiet charm. Once in Shoreline Park, the dirt and gravel trails lead along the waterfront where there are informative signs explaining how to spot the abundant wildlife there. More trails in Baylands Preserve lead back to Palo Alto and through the downtown and finally back to the campus.

Starting Point

Start the ride at the football stadium parking lot on the campus of Stanford University. To get there, take Highway 101 to Palo Alto and get off at the exit for Embarcadero Road. Follow Embarcadero across El Camino Real into the Stanford campus. Embarcadero Road becomes Galvez Street after crossing El Camino Real. There is plenty of parking at the stadium near the Sport Shop.

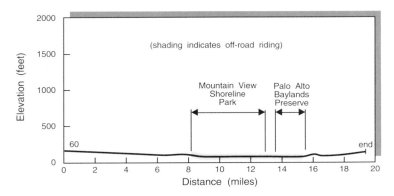

(shading indicates off-road riding)

Mile Markers

0.0 From the stadium parking lot, turn LEFT onto Galvez Street, heading toward the middle of the campus.

0.1 Turn LEFT onto East Campus Drive.

0.5 Turn LEFT onto Serra Street.

1.0 Turn LEFT onto El Camino Real.

1.2 Turn RIGHT onto Churchill Avenue.

1.8 Turn RIGHT onto Waverley Street, LEFT onto Coleridge Avenue and RIGHT onto Cowper Street.

3.4 Turn LEFT onto Loma Verde Avenue and RIGHT onto Middlefield Road.

5.2 Bear LEFT onto Old Middlefield Way.

5.7 Turn LEFT onto Rengstorff Avenue.

8.0 Enter Shoreline Park and follow the bike path along the right side of the road.

9.0 Turn RIGHT on bike path just after you cross footbridge and then turn RIGHT again immediately.

9.8 Bear RIGHT at trail split.

10.1 Turn RIGHT to head out onto dirt trail on levee.

12.3 Continue past the gate at the end of the bike path.

12.7 Turn RIGHT onto the road.

12.9 Continue STRAIGHT at Embarcadero Road intersection.

13.4 Turn LEFT onto the gravel bike path just beyond the airport to enter Palo Alto Baylands Preserve.

13.7 Continue past gate and turn RIGHT to stay on the dirt path. Continue around the airport and past the golf course.

14.6 Continue past gate and bear LEFT.

15.2 Bear LEFT to get off the bike path and continue through the parking lot.

15.5 Turn RIGHT onto Embarcadero Road.

16.0 Just after freeway overpass, turn RIGHT onto St. Francis and then LEFT onto Channing Avenue.

17.4 Turn RIGHT onto Gunda Street and then LEFT onto Homer Avenue.

18.2 Turn RIGHT onto Waverley Avenue and LEFT onto University Avenue in central Palo Alto.

18.7 Cross El Camino Real and enter the university on Palm Drive.

19.0 Turn LEFT onto Arboretum Street.

19.3 Turn RIGHT onto Galvez Street.

19.5 End of the ride back at the stadium.

Further Information

Mountain View Shoreline Park: (415) 903-6392

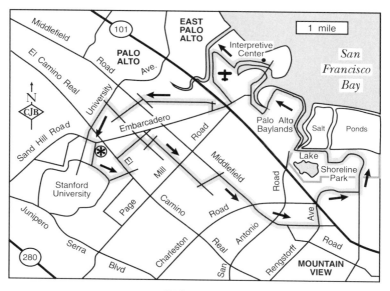

Ride No. 18

19   San Bruno
Sweeney Ridge

Region: *Peninsula*
Difficulty Rating: *Moderate*
Skill Level: *Intermediate*
Elevation Gain: *1600 feet*

Total Distance: *12 miles*
Off-Road Distance: *5 miles*
Riding Time: *2 hours*
Total Calories: *700*

About the Ride

On November 4, 1769, the expedition of the Spanish explorer, Captain Gaspar de Portolá, in search of Monterey Bay, climbed from the coast to what is today Sweeney Ridge. From that vantage point, his party beheld the valley below and the present-day San Francisco Bay. Not realizing the importance of his discovery, Portolá and his group camped by a small lagoon, now covered over by San Andreas Lake, and attempted to get around the bay. Unsuccessful in doing that, he eventually found Monterey Bay in the following year. In 1773, subsequent Spanish expeditions charted the San Francisco Bay and established San Francisco. From the top of Sweeney Ridge, where there is a small marker commemorating the Portolá expedition, you can see San Andreas Lake to the east, along with the San Francisco Watershed, the Bay, and Mount Diablo, and to the west, Pacifica and the ocean shoreline.

The route starts at the Skyline College campus, located nearby. It leads through nearby residential neighborhoods to Sneath Lane. At the end of Sneath Lane is a paved trail, also named Sneath Lane, leading to Sweeney Ridge. Very steep in places, the trail climbs about 600 feet to get to the top of the ridge, where there is a small marker commemorating the Portolá expedition on the unpaved Sweeney Ridge Trail. After proceeding out and back along Sweeney Ridge Trail, the route will take you down the other side of the ridge along the Baquaino Trail to Pacifica. This trail is also unpaved and is very steep. Once in Pacifica, you will follow Highway 1 a short distance north and then return to the campus by climbing up Sharp Park Road.

Road surfaces are paved, except for about 5 miles on dirt trails with some very steep downhill sections. Some traffic can be expected on Highway 1 for about half a mile. Two climbs are required, with one very steep section on Sneath Lane.

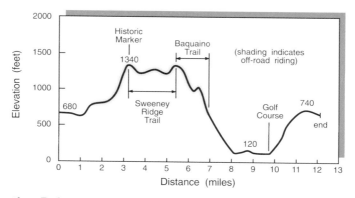

Starting Point

Skyline College in San Bruno is the starting point for the ride. There is plenty of parking on the campus, but during the week you must be careful to avoid parking in areas requiring a permit. To get to the campus from the north, get off Highway 280 at Sneath Lane and follow Sneath Lane west to Skyline Boulevard. Turn right on Skyline Boulevard and proceed about ½-mile to the campus. From the south, exit Highway 280 at the Skyline Boulevard and Pacifica off ramp. Follow Skyline Boulevard for about 2.5 miles to the campus. Start the mileage from the athletic field in the center of the campus.

Mile Markers

0.0 Proceed out of the campus along College Drive toward Skyline Boulevard.

0.5 Turn RIGHT onto Longview Drive

0.6 Turn LEFT onto Moreland Drive.

0.8 Turn LEFT onto Riverside Drive.

0.9 Turn RIGHT onto Sneath Lane.

1.6 Continue STRAIGHT into Golden Gate National Recreation Area at the end of Sneath Lane and head toward Sweeney Ridge.

3.2 At the top of the ridge, turn LEFT onto unpaved Sweeney Ridge Trail.

3.3 Historical marker is located on the hilltop to the left of the trail.

4.4 At the gate at the end of Sweeney Ridge Trail, turn around and return the way you came.

5.4 Turn LEFT onto Baquaino Trail and prepare for steep descent.

6.4 Continue past the gate and then turn LEFT toward Fassler Avenue.

6.9 Continue past the gate onto Fassler Avenue.

8.2 Turn RIGHT onto Highway 1.

8.8 Cross over Highway 1 to use the bike path on the west side of the roadway.

9.1 Follow the bike route signs to avoid this section of the highway. You will follow parallel to the highway on Bradford Way along the golf course.

9.8 Turn RIGHT onto Sharp Park Road and cross over highway.

11.1 Turn RIGHT onto College Drive toward the campus.

11.5 Enter the campus and turn RIGHT to loop around.

12.1 End of the ride at the athletic field.

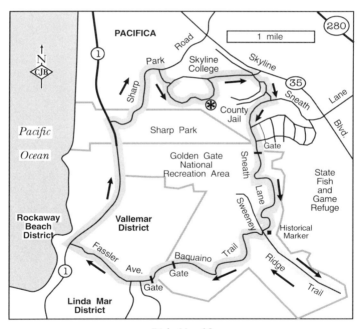

Ride No. 19

20   Woodside

Purisima Creek Redwoods Open Space Preserve

Region: *Peninsula*
Difficulty Rating: *Difficult*
Skill Level: *Advanced*
Elevation Gain: *1600 feet*

Total Distance: *9 miles*
Off-Road Distance: *7 miles*
Riding Time: *2-3 hours*
Total Calories: *1000*

About the Ride

The headwaters for Purisima Creek form on the upper reaches of the western slope of the Santa Cruz Mountains. Following a path through lush redwood forests, the creek works its way to the ocean at a point about 4 miles south of Half Moon Bay. The Purisima Creek Open Space Preserve consists of about 2,500 acres of magnificent public land, open for the use of hikers, runners, equestrians, and bicyclists.

This ride encompasses nearly the entire preserve and allows the cyclist to experience the full range of pristine beauty available there. The ride begins with a steady descent through deep redwood forests, followed by a fairly flat section along Purisima Creek and includes bridge crossings over the creek in several places. The return to the top of the mountain ridge is along Harkins Fire Trail. Although very steep in some places, this route affords some spectacular views toward Half Moon Bay on the coast. Once back at Skyline Boulevard, the return to the starting point is along a relatively flat section of Skyline Boulevard.

Most of the ride is on dirt fire roads through the preserve. Some very steep sections may require you to walk your bike a small amount. There is considerabe poison oak in the area, so be very careful not to touch anything suspicious-looking.

Starting Point

Begin the ride at the Purisima Creek trailhead, located about 0.4 miles from the intersection of Skyline Boulevard and Kings Mountain Road above the town of Woodside. To get there, take the Woodside Road (Highway 84) exit from Highway 280 and proceed west toward Woodside. Continue through Woodside and turn right on Kings Mountain Road, following it all the way to the top, at Skyline Boulevard. Turn right on Skyline Boulevard and look for the Purisima Creek trailhead on the left side.

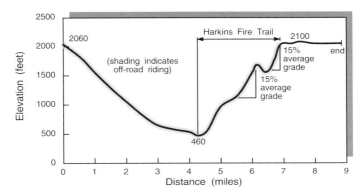

Mile Markers

0.0 From the trailhead, enter the park and follow Redwood Trail toward Purisima Creek Trail.

0.1 Turn LEFT onto Purisima Creek Trail.

1.9 Trail intersection on the right side.

2.3 Cross wooden bridge.

2.9 Grabtown Gulch Trail intersection on the left side.

3.0 Cross second bridge.

3.3 Borden Hatch Mill Trail intersection on the left.

4.2 Turn RIGHT onto Harkins Ridge Trail, cross bridge and then turn RIGHT again to stay on Harkins Ridge Trail.

5.1 Steep uphill sections ahead.

5.8 Soda Gulch Trail intersection on the right.

6.1 Bear LEFT to stay on trail and begin single-track section.

6.6 Turn RIGHT toward Skyline parking.

6.8 Exit preserve and turn RIGHT onto Skyline Boulevard.

8.8 Back at the start point.

Further Information

Midpeninsula Regional Open Space District: (415) 949-5500

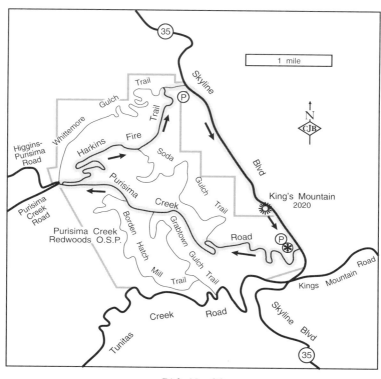

Ride No. 20

Looking toward the ocean from Harkins Fire Trail.

21 Loma Mar
Old Haul Road

Region: *Peninsula*
Difficulty Rating: *Easy*
Skill Level: *Beginner*
Elevation Gain: *800 feet*

Total Distance: *16 miles*
Off-Road Distance: *12 miles*
Riding Time: *2 hours*
Total Calories: *700*

About the Ride

The lumber demand created by the California Gold Rush of 1849 was met by the seemingly endless redwood forests of the Santa Cruz Mountains. Getting the timber out of the forests, however, required the construction of roads and railways. One of these, no longer in use for logging, is today called Old Haul Road and is located within Pescadero Creek County Park. Following a route through the park, it extends from Loma Mar, just east of Pescadero, to Portola State Park. A recreational trail for use by hikers, cyclists, and equestrians, Old Haul Road, by virtue of its former use as a railroad bed, does not present the extreme steep terrain usually associated with mountain biking. With the exception of a few short steep sections, the grade is a gentle one and the trails are all very well-marked.

This easy route takes you from Loma Mar into Pescadero Creek County Park and follows Old Haul Road all the way to the park headquarters of Portola State Park. The return is along the same route.

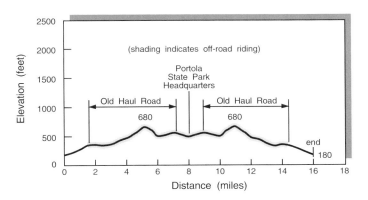

Starting Point

Start the ride in Loma Mar, about 6 miles east of Pescadero, at the Loma Mar Store. To get there, take the Woodside Road (Highway 84) exit off of Interstate Highway 280 and follow Woodside Road through Woodside over the mountain and down into La Honda. Turn left just past La Honda on Pescadero Road and follow it all the way to Loma Mar. The Loma Mar Store is the only public structure in Loma Mar, which would be easy to miss were it not for the store. Park anywhere nearby and begin the ride at the store.

Mile Markers

0.0 From the Loma Mar store, proceed EAST on Pescadero Road.

0.1 Turn RIGHT onto Wurr Road.

1.6 Turn RIGHT into Pescadero County Park on Old Haul Road. Continue past gate onto wide dirt trail.

2.2 Continue past gate.

2.4 Pomponio Trail intersection on the left side.

3.0 Towne Trail intersection on the left side.

3.5 Butano Ridge Loop Trail intersection on the right.

5.9 Bridge Trail intersection on the left side.

6.0 Butano Ridge Loop Trail intersection on the right.

7.1 Turn LEFT off Old Haul Road into Portola State Park and begin steep descent. Look for the remains of the historic Iverson cabin at the bottom of the hill.

8.0 Park headquarters on the left side. Return back the way you came.

8.9 Turn RIGHT onto Old Haul Road, heading back toward Loma Mar.

14.4 Turn RIGHT at the end of the trail onto Wurr Road.

14.6 Turn LEFT onto Pescadero Road.

16.3 End of the ride at Loma Mar store.

Further Information

San Mateo County Memorial Park: (415) 879-0212
Portola State Park: (415) 948-9098
Pescadero Creek County Park: (415) 363-4026

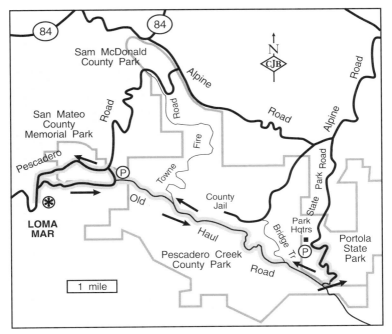

Ride No. 21

Courtesy of Santa Cruz Mountains Natural History Association

IVERSON CABIN

22 Palo Alto
Russian Ridge Open Space Preserve

Region: *Peninsula*
Difficulty Rating: *Moderate*
Skill Level: *Intermediate*
Elevation Gain: *1300 feet*

Total Distance: *11 miles*
Off-Road Distance: *10 miles*
Riding Time: *2-3 hours*
Total Calories: *800*

About the Ride

At the top of the Santa Cruz Mountain range high above Palo Alto, lie four individual open space preserves: Russian Ridge, Coal Creek, Monte Bello, and Skyline Ridge. When considered in total, they form one of the largest regions in the Bay Area in which bicyclists, hikers, and equestrians can enjoy the beauty of undeveloped country. The junction of Page Mill Road, Skyline Boulevard, and Alpine Road provides a convenient jumping off place for bike rides on the rolling hills of each preserve.

This ride tours both Russian Ridge and Coal Creek, covering almost 11 miles of trails through mountain meadows and coastal forests. Substantial climbing can be expected, since the trails follow along rolling mountain ridges for most of the route. Whereas wide fire trails predominate in Russian Ridge, there are some narrow single-tracks to contend with in Coal Creek. A little more than one mile of road riding is necessary to connect between the preserves.

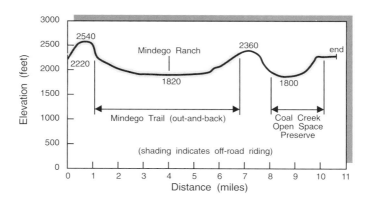

Starting Point

Start the ride at the parking lot for Russian Ridge Open Space Preserve. To get there take Highway 280 to Palo Alto and get off at the exit for Page Mill Road. Follow Page Mill Road west all the way to the top at Skyline Boulevard. Cross over to Alpine Road and look for the parking lot just on the other side of Skyline Boulevard.

Mile Markers

0.0 Proceed NORTH out of the parking lot on Ridge Trail, heading toward Borel Hill.

0.5 Bear RIGHT to stay on Ridge Trail.

0.8 Bear RIGHT at the trail junction at the crest of the hill.

1.2 Turn LEFT onto Mindego Ridge Trail.

1.5 Alder Springs Trail intersection on the right side.

3.0 Turn RIGHT onto the fire road to stay on Mindego Ridge Trail.

4.1 Turn AROUND at the end of the trail at the Mindego Ranch and return the way you came.

5.2 Turn LEFT to continue on Mindego Ridge Trail.

6.8 Continue STRAIGHT at the intersection with Ridge Trail, heading toward Skyline Boulevard.

6.9 Turn LEFT onto Skyline Boulevard.

7.5 Turn RIGHT onto Crazy Pete's Road. This road is small and easy to miss.

7.8 Bear RIGHT at the junction at the end of the paved road.

7.9 Bear RIGHT to enter Coal Creek Preserve at gate "CC04." Turn RIGHT immediately after the gate to stay on Crazy Pete's Road, heading toward Alpine Road.

8.1 Bear RIGHT at the intersection with Valley View Trail on the left to stay on Crazy Pete's Road.

8.9 Turn RIGHT after the barrier onto Alpine Road.

10.1 Turn RIGHT after the barrier onto Page Mill Road.

10.7 Cross Skyline Boulevard.

10.8 End of the ride at Russian Ridge.

Further Information

Midpeninsula Regional Open Space District: (415) 949-5500

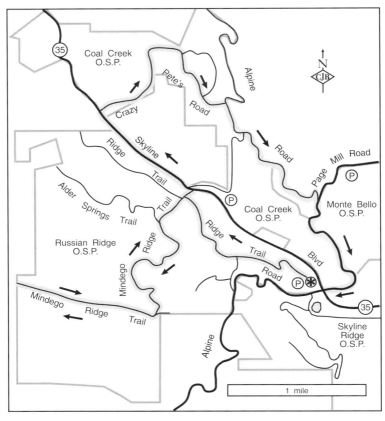

Ride No. 22

Along Mindego Ridge Trail.

23 **Palo Alto**
Skyline Ridge Open Space Preserve

Region: *Peninsula*
Difficulty Rating: *Moderate*
Skill Level: *Intermediate*
Elevation Gain: *1200 feet*

Total Distance: *7 miles*
Off-Road Distance: *6 miles*
Riding Time: *2 hours*
Total Calories: *700*

About the Ride

Skyline Ridge Open Space and the Upper part of Monte Bello Open Space form the area covered by this ride. Located high in the mountains above Palo Alto, these preserves are just a portion of the recreational land owned by the citizens of California and administered by the Midpeninsula Regional Open Space District.

The route begins in the parking lot for Russian Ridge Open Space (located adjacent to Skyline Ridge) and leads immediately past a small pond and then up a hill into Skyline Ridge. Views of Monte Bello at the top of the hill are followed by the descent toward Horseshoe Lake. After passing the lake, and then going through the parking lot for Skyline Ridge, the route will lead you into Monte Bello, the upper watershed of Stevens Creek.

The trail through Monte Bello, while narrow at times, will take you down into the canyon and then follows the Canyon Trail back up the hill. After passing the main parking lot for Monte Bello, the route will then lead you through a meadow, down along a steep single-track and across a stream before going back out of Monte Bello the way you came in. The final return to the start point is along Skyline Boulevard.

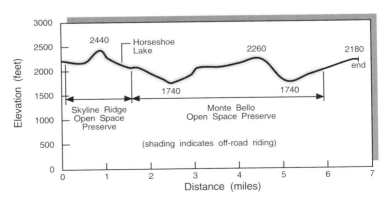

Starting Point

Start the ride at the parking lot for Russian Ridge Open Space Preserve. To get there take Highway 280 to Palo Alto and get off at the exit for Page Mill Road. Follow Page Mill Road west all the way to the top at Skyline Boulevard. Cross over to Alpine Road and look for the parking lot just on the other side of Skyline Boulevard.

Mile Markers

0.0 Cross Alpine Road to get to the trailhead into Skyline Ridge.

0.1 Cross barrier to get on Alternate Ridge Trail toward Horseshoe Lake and Skyline parking.

0.2 At Alpine Pond, bear RIGHT to stay on bicycle-only trail around the lake and then turn LEFT on the paved road.

0.4 Dirt trail begins just after private residences.

0.6 Turn LEFT to stay on Alternate Ridge Trail.

1.0 Continue STRAIGHT at the major trail intersection.

1.4 Horseshoe Lake on the right side.

1.5 Continue past the barrier and through the equestrian parking lot and turn LEFT onto the trail leading to the main parking area.

1.7 Just past the main parking area, turn LEFT and cross Skyline Boulevard to reach the trailhead into Monte Bello Open Space (gate "MB06"). Just past the gate, bear LEFT and follow the trail as it runs parallel to the road.

2.1 Continue STRAIGHT at trail intersection on the left.

2.3 Continue STRAIGHT toward Canyon Trail at another trail intersection on the left.

2.9 Turn LEFT onto Canyon Trail, heading toward Page Mill Road.

3.6 Continue STRAIGHT toward Los Trancos at the trail intersection on the left.

3.8 Turn LEFT just before the gate and stay on this trail as it follows parallel to the road.

4.0 Continue THROUGH the parking area for Monte Bello and continue on the trail parallel to the road.

4.5 Bear LEFT at the trail split toward Skyline Boulevard.

5.6 Turn RIGHT at the end of the trail and continue toward Skyline Boulevard.

5.9 Exit Monte Bello and turn RIGHT onto Skyline Boulevard.

6.6 End of the ride at Russian Ridge parking area.

Further Information

Midpeninsula Regional Open Space District: (415) 949-5500

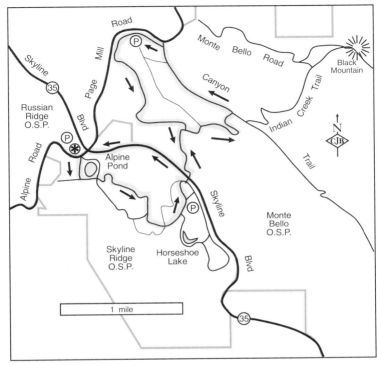

Ride No. 23

The Stevens Creek Watershed, as seen from Skyline Ridge.

24   Saratoga

Saratoga Gap and Long Ridge Preserves

Region: *Peninsula*
Difficulty Rating: *Moderate*
Skill Level: *Intermediate*
Elevation Gain: *900 feet*

Total Distance: *10 miles*
Off-Road Distance: *10 miles*
Riding Time: *2 hours*
Total Calories: *650*

About the Ride

At the top of the mountains above the town of Saratoga lie Saratoga Gap and Long Ridge Open Space Preserves and Skyline County Park. The areas all connect to each other and contain wonderful mountain biking trails with great variety and fabulous views.

The Saratoga Gap trailhead is the kick-off place for the ride and is located near the intersection of Skyline Boulevard (Highway 35) and Congress Springs Road (Highway 9). You will travel the 2-mile distance through Saratoga Gap to Long Ridge Open Space along a narrow single-track trail through heavy forest. This section has some rather steep drop-offs to one side, so you would be wise to use extra caution here.

After passing through Saratoga Gap and crossing over Skyline Boulevard, the trail then takes you into Long Ridge Preserve. Open meadows with expansive views to the west are interspersed with thick woods. You will ride along both wide fire roads and narrow single-track. At the northernmost end of the preserve, the route will lead you first down a hill and then along Peters Creek, lush with ferns and heavy forest and cool even in the hot summer months. After passing a small pond, you will then climb up a fairly steep single-track with sharp switchbacks before returning to Saratoga Gap the way you came.

While the ride itself is relatively short and the total elevation gain is reasonably modest, the trails are quite narrow in some places and frequently have steep drop-offs to the side. Sharp switchbacks should be taken with care and some walking may be required.

Starting Point

Start the ride at Saratoga Gap, located at the intersection of Congress Springs Road (Highway 9) and Skyline Boulevard (Highway 35), about 7 miles west of Saratoga. To get there, take Interstate 280 and get off at the Saratoga Avenue exit. Follow Saratoga Avenue west until you reach the town of Saratoga. Continue through Saratoga on

Highway 9 (Big Basin Way, which later becomes Congress Springs Road) to the top of the mountain at the intersection with Skyline Boulevard. Park in the vista point parking lot and look for the trailhead across Congress Springs Road.

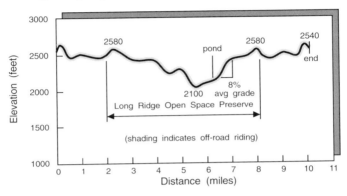

Mile Markers

0.0 Proceed through gate into Saratoga Gap Open Space Preserve on Saratoga Gap Trail

1.7 Continue STRAIGHT across dirt road.

2.0 Continue STRAIGHT across Skyline Boulevard and enter Long Ridge Open Space Preserve on fire road.

2.1 Turn RIGHT to stay on fire road.

2.3 Bear LEFT at trail split and follow single-track across meadow and through woods.

2.5 Turn LEFT to get back onto fire road.

3.1 Bear RIGHT at trail split to follow Ridge Trail. (Ward Road is to the left.)

3.3 Turn LEFT onto wide fire road (this is Ward Road) toward Long Ridge Road.

3.4 Continue STRAIGHT ahead to get on Long Ridge Road. (Ward Road continues to the left.)

3.9 Turn RIGHT toward Peters Creek Trail. (Gate out of preserve is straight ahead — private property — bikes not permitted.)

4.9 Continue STRAIGHT ahead at trail intersection on right (Peters Creek Trail Loop).

5.4 Continue STRAIGHT ahead onto Peters Creek Trail. Grizzly Flat parking area to the left.

5.8 Turn LEFT on fire road toward Long Ridge Road. (Peters Creek Trail goes to the right.)

6.4 Turn RIGHT to stay on Ridge Trail. Cross bridge and continue on single-track uphill with switchbacks.

6.9 Turn LEFT onto Ward Road. (Long Ridge Road goes to the right.)

7.0 Turn RIGHT onto single-track trail.

7.2 Turn LEFT onto fire road.

7.8 Turn RIGHT onto single-track trail.

8.0 Turn RIGHT onto fire road.

8.1 Turn LEFT to stay on fire road toward Skyline Boulevard gate.

8.2 Continue STRAIGHT across Skyline Boulevard and get back on Saratoga Gap Trail in Skyline County Park.

8.6 Continue STRAIGHT across dirt road.

10.2 End of the ride back at Saratoga Gap.

Further Information

Midpeninsula Regional Open Space District: (415) 949-5500

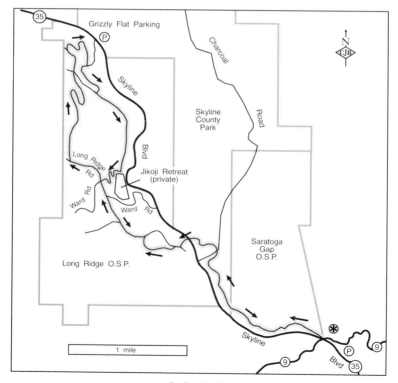

Ride No. 24

25 Portola Valley
Alpine Road and Windy Hill Loop

Region: *Peninsula*
Difficulty Rating: *Difficult*
Skill Level: *Intermediate*
Elevation Gain: *2200 feet*

Total Distance: *18 miles*
Off-Road Distance: *6 miles*
Riding Time: *3 hours*
Total Calories: *1200*

About the Ride

The Alpine Inn — fondly remembered by the locals as "Rossotti's" — serves as the starting point for this ride. Alpine Road is a smooth road with a wide bike lane, leading through beautiful Portola Valley, favored by the many cyclists and equestrians usually found here on weekends. A relatively little-known route takes what normally would be a road bike ride and changes it dramatically into a wonderful mountain biking experience.

The route first takes you to the end of the paved portion up Alpine Road and then proceeds on the old section, along a dirt fire trail leading to the top of the mountain at Page Mill Road. The trail is wide and generally smooth, although bumps are common in some sections, especially after a rainfall.

At the end of the climb along the dirt road, a short section on Page Mill Road will take you to Skyline Boulevard at the top of the mountain. Just across Skyline Boulevard, you will once again hit the dirt and climb again for a short section through Russian Ridge Open Space Preserve, after which it's back to the pavement on Skyline Boulevard for about 4 miles to get to Windy Hill Open Space Preserve.

In Windy Hill, there is only one trail open to bikes and that one, Spring Ridge Trail, takes you all the way down the mountain. While you pass through the open meadows on the mountainside, be sure to stop periodically to savor the views of the valley ahead and below you. The end of the trail will dump you onto Portola Road, where you can join up with the "roadies" for the return to Alpine Inn.

The main climbing is along the dirt section of Alpine Road. While not terribly steep, the 8.5% average grade is sustained over several miles and will certainly get your heart pounding. Single-track trails in Russian Ridge provide challenge to your mountain bike skills, while the downhill through Windy Hill will exercise your forearms, as your brakes will be on most of the time.

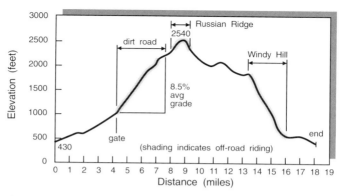

(shading indicates off-road riding)

Starting Point

The ride starts in Portola Valley at the intersection of Alpine Road and Arastradero Road. To get there, take the Alpine Road exit from Interstate Highway 280 and proceed west on Alpine Road for about 1 mile to the intersection with Arastradero Road. Start the ride at the Alpine Inn restaurant, but be sure to park at the far reaches of the parking lot in order to permit their customers easy access to the restaurant.

Mile Markers

0.0 Proceed WEST on Alpine Road away from Highway 280.

1.1 Continue STRAIGHT at the intersection with Portola Road on the right.

4.5 Turn RIGHT off the paved road to begin the unpaved section of Alpine Road. You will recognize this point by the steep hill ahead of you through the portals on the paved road and by the gate off the road on the right marking the start of the dirt road.

7.1 Turn RIGHT onto Page Mill Road, just beyond the gate at the end of the dirt section.

7.8 Continue STRAIGHT across Skyline Boulevard and turn RIGHT immediately into the parking area for Russian Ridge Open Space Preserve. Get on the Ridge Trail, heading north.

8.8 Crest of the trail (2,540-foot elevation) — great views in all directions.

9.2 Turn RIGHT at trail intersection toward Skyline Boulevard gate.

9.3 Turn LEFT onto Skyline Boulevard.

11.6 First entrance for Windy Hill on the right side — bikes not permitted.

12.4 Second entrance for Windy Hill on right side.

13.0 Main entrance for Windy Hill on right side.

13.4 Turn RIGHT into Windy Hill Open Space Preserve at gate, "WH01." Follow the Spring Ridge Trail toward Portola Road. This is the only trail on which bikes are allowed. Enjoy the superb views of Palo Alto, Stanford University, and the Bay.

16.0 Exit past the gate and turn RIGHT onto a gravel road.

16.1 Turn RIGHT onto Portola Road.

17.0 Turn LEFT onto Alpine Road.

18.1 End of the ride at the Alpine Inn.

Further Information

Midpeninsula Regional Open Spact District: (415) 949-5500

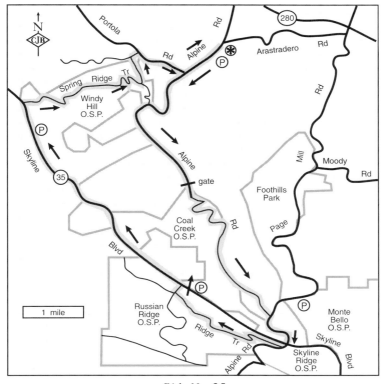

Ride No. 25

The East Bay

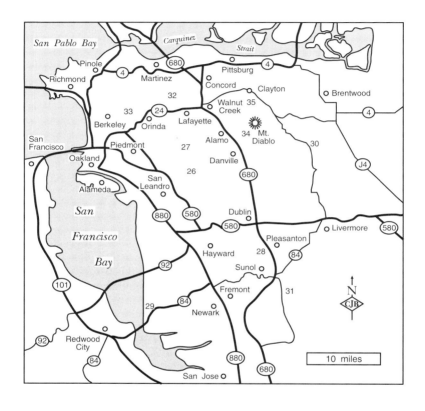

26 San Leandro
Chabot Regional Park

Region: *East Bay*	**Total Distance:** *20 miles*
Difficulty Rating: *Difficult*	**Off-Road Distance:** *20 miles*
Skill Level: *Intermediate*	**Riding Time:** *3-4 hours*
Elevation Gain: *2200 feet*	**Total Calories:** *1000*

About the Ride

This mountain bike ride covers 20 miles of trails and completely traverses Anthony Chabot Regional Park, located near San Leandro. The route begins at one of the rear accesses into the park, the MacDonald Staging Area along Redwood Road, and immediately climbs on a steep grade along MacDonald Trail. Expansive views at the crest are brief, as the trail drops sharply into the valley below. Passing through Grass Valley along the Brandon Trail, you will often encounter grazing cattle at close range. After a short climb at the end of the Grass Valley, the trail then descends and follows a paved path leading around Lake Chabot. There is usually more activity around this part of the park, since the lake offers more activities and attracts families with children on weekends.

After more than 5 miles riding along the edge of the lake, you will cross a narrow wooden bridge, where you will need to walk your bike. Continue on along the far side of the lake, where the dirt trails resume. A steep climb of about 800 feet in elevation gain takes you away from the lake and back into the more remote sections of the park, leading you through some camping areas along the crest of the mountains. After riding along the ridge for a short distance, a steep descent back into Grass Valley is followed by a climb back up MacDonald Trail and the final descent back to the starting point.

While there are lots of hills to climb in Chabot Park, the trails are wide and usually smooth. Livestock may be present, but they are normally quite passive and more wary of cyclists than vice versa.

Starting Point

Start the ride at the MacDonald Staging Area for Chabot Regional Park on Redwood Road. To get there, take Highway 13, the Warren Freeway, and get off at the exit for Redwood Road. Follow Redwood Road east up into the hills and continue past the intersection with Skyline Boulevard for about 2 miles to the MacDonald Staging Area on the right side.

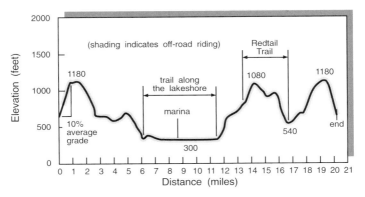

Mile Markers

0.0 Proceed into Chabot Park on MacDonald Trail on the left side of the parking area.

1.1 Turn LEFT to stay on MacDonald Trail.

2.5 Turn RIGHT just after livestock gate toward Bort Meadow and Grass Valley.

2.6 Turn LEFT onto the wide trail at the bottom of the hill.

2.7 Turn RIGHT toward Brandon Trail, then LEFT onto Brandon Trail.

4.1 Turn RIGHT to get on Jackson Grade.

4.6 Skyline Boulevard gate on the right side. Do not go through the gate, but continue ahead on Goldenrod Trail.

5.6 Turn LEFT off paved section onto continuation of Goldenrod Trail.

6.0 Continue STRAIGHT on Bass Cove Trail toward marina.

7.0 Continue STRAIGHT across service road and begin West Shore Trail.

8.7 Just past the marina on the left side, turn LEFT in picnic area, cross wooden bridge and turn LEFT onto trail continuing along lake shore. This is East Shore Trail.

10.4 Begin dirt trail.

10.6 Turn LEFT to cross narrow wooden bridge, the turn LEFT onto Honker Bay Trail along the lake shore.

11.7 Begin climbing.

12.4 Continue STRAIGHT on paved road through campground.

13.0 Just past the park entrance booth, get on Towhee Trail running parallel to right side of road.

13.4 Turn LEFT onto Brandon Trail.

13.6 Turn RIGHT onto Redtail Trail, just before the road.

14.0 Cross road and continue on Redtail Trail.

14.8   Bear RIGHT to stay on Redtail Trail and cross road.

15.1   Turn RIGHT on road and then turn LEFT to get on continuation of Redtail Trail.

16.7   Turn RIGHT onto Grass Valley Trail.

17.6   Continue past gate toward Bort Meadow and then turn RIGHT onto small trail up the hill toward MacDonald Trail.

17.7   Turn LEFT onto MacDonald Trail.

20.3   Back at the start point.

Further Information

East Bay Regional Park District: (510) 531-9300

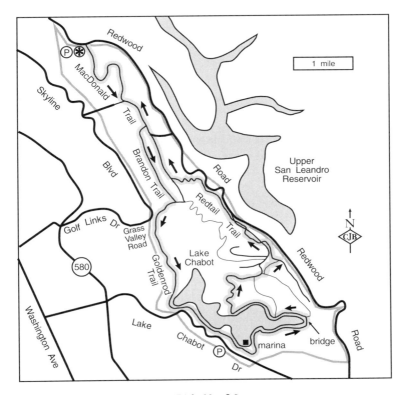

Ride No. 26

27 San Leandro
Redwood Regional Park

Region: *East Bay*	**Total Distance:** *10 miles*
Difficulty Rating: *Moderate*	**Off-Road Distance:** *10 miles*
Skill Level: *Intermediate*	**Riding Time:** *2 hours*
Elevation Gain: *1200 feet*	**Total Calories:** *700*

About the Ride

Redwood Regional Park is today home to giant redwood trees descended from original growth trees logged long ago. The park consists of a central valley surrounded by mountains and is rich with trails for hiking, biking, and equestrian use. As is the case with all parks administered by the East Bay Regional Park District, bikes are restricted to fire roads and must yield at all times to both hikers and equestrians.

This route follows around the park periphery along the mountain ridges, affording spectacular views in all directions. Beginning at a trail-head near the park headquarters, the route immediately climbs on a very steep grade along the West Ridge Trail. Expect to walk your bike up the steep sections and console yourself as you do this with the fact that once up onto the ridge, the remainder of the ride will require little or no climbing.

From the west ridge, the equestrian center can be seen below. Continuing past the Roberts Recreation Area and the Archery Range at the high point of the ride, 1,540 feet above sea level, the first scenes of the valley, in the central part of the park, can be seen. After Skyline Gate, the East Ridge Trail allows you to cruise on a gentle downhill grade to the intersection for Canyon Trail, which takes you on a steep descent to the valley floor and the paved service road leading back to the starting point.

The route generally follows wide unpaved fire trails with loose stones. Some very steep sections in the beginning will require all but the strongest riders to walk their bikes.

Starting Point

Start the ride at the main entrance for Redwood Regional Park on Redwood Road. To get there, take Highway 13, the Warren Freeway, and get off at the exit for Redwood Road. Follow Redwood Road east up into the hills and continue past the intersection with Skyline Boulevard for about 2 miles to the entrance for Redwood Regional Park on the left side. Park anywhere and start the ride at the first trailhead on the left side of the road entering the park, at the Fern Hut/Mill Site, Fishway Interpretive Center.

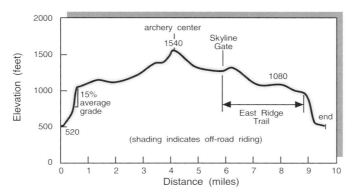

Mile Markers

0.0 Proceed out of the parking area into Redwood Regional Park toward Middle Trail and turn RIGHT onto Middle Trail.

0.1 Turn LEFT onto West Ridge Trail.

0.4 Golden Spike Trail intersection on the left side.

0.6 Toyon Trail intersection on the left side.

0.9 Orchard Trail intersection on the right, followed by Tate Trail on the left.

1.2 Turn LEFT onto Baccharis Trail.

1.7 Turn LEFT onto Dunn Trail.

2.8 Bear RIGHT to get on Graham Trail.

3.4 Trail to Roberts Park on the left side.

3.9 Turn LEFT to get back onto West Ridge Trail.

4.1 Archery Center on the right side.

4.2 Continue past the gate to stay on West Ridge Trail.

4.6 Moon Gate on the left side.

4.8 Tres Sendas Trail intersection on the right side.

5.3 French Trail intersection on the right side.

5.9 Continue straight ahead at Skyline Gate and begin East Ridge Trail.

7.2 Prince Road on the right side.

8.9 Turn RIGHT onto Canyon Trail.

9.3 Turn LEFT onto the paved road at the end of the trail.

9.6 Back at the start point.

Further Information

East Bay Regional Park District: (510) 531-9300

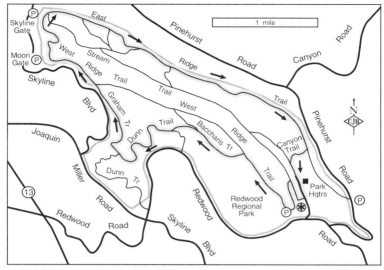

Ride No. 27

The view into Redwood Regional Park.

28 Pleasanton
Pleasanton Ridge

Region: *East Bay*	**Total Distance:** *9 miles*
Difficulty Rating: *Difficult*	**Off-Road Distance:** *9 miles*
Skill Level: *Intermediate*	**Riding Time:** *2 hours*
Elevation Gain: *1600 feet*	**Total Calories:** *900*

About the Ride

Just west of the charming town of Pleasanton lies Pleasanton Ridge Regional Park. The quiet and peaceful atmosphere of the park stands in sharp contrast to the hectic pace of car traffic just a few miles away on busy Highway 680. Following wide fire roads, this ride has plenty of very steep terrain. Even along the crest, expect to shift gears frequently as you go up and down some rather steep slopes.

Leaving the parking area on Oak Tree Trail, the route climbs immediately toward the intersection with Ridgeline Trail. Grassy slopes and oak-dotted hillsides are the dominant features of the park as Ridgeline Trail continues its climb skyward. Along the ridge, panoramic vistas toward the east into the Livermore Valley come into view. A conveniently placed picnic table beckons you to rest and to savor the moment.

The open landscape of Ridgeline Trail changes abruptly as you pass through a heavily wooded section just before getting back on Ridgeline Trail. The return is initially back along Ridgeline Trail and then along Thermalito Trail, with views of the west side of the ridge and Kilkare Canyon, far below. After passing some old ranch buildings, you descend back to the parking lot along Oak Tree Trail.

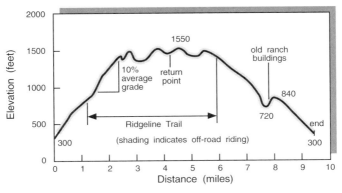

Starting Point

Start the ride at the Oak Tree Staging Area for Pleasanton Regional Park on Foothill Road, just north of Sunol. To get there, take Highway 680 toward Pleasanton and get off at Bernal Avenue. Proceed west on Bernal Avenue for a short distance and then south on Foothill Road for about 3 miles to Pleasanton Ridge Regional Park, where there is plenty of parking.

Mile Markers

0.0 Proceed out of the parking area away from the road on Oak Tree Trail.

0.6 Continue STRAIGHT at intersection with trail to Sycamore Groves on the right side.

1.2 Turn RIGHT and pass through gate on Oak Tree Trail, then turn RIGHT again to get on Ridgeline Trail and begin steep climb.

1.4 Bear RIGHT to stay on Ridgeline Trail.

1.8 Olive Trail intersection on the left side.

2.3 Trail toward Thermalito Trail on the left side.

2.5 Thermalito Trail intersection on the left side.

2.8 Continue past gate, then bear RIGHT to stay on Ridgeline Trail. Steep downhill section.

2.9 Turn LEFT to stay on Ridgeline Trail.

3.1 Enter Augustine Bernal Park area.

3.7 Continue past gate and turn RIGHT onto unmarked trail. This will ultimately re-connect to Ridgeline Trail.

4.2 Turn LEFT onto Ridgeline Trail and head back.

4.6 Continue past gate and stay on Ridgeline Trail.

5.5 Continue past another gate.

5.9 Turn RIGHT onto Thermalito Trail.

7.7 Turn LEFT onto Oak Tree Trail.

8.0 Continue STRAIGHT across Ridgeline Trail, pass gate, and turn LEFT to stay on Oak Tree Trail.

9.4 Back at the start point.

Further Information

East Bay Regional Park District: (510) 531-9300

Bay Area Mountain Bike Trails

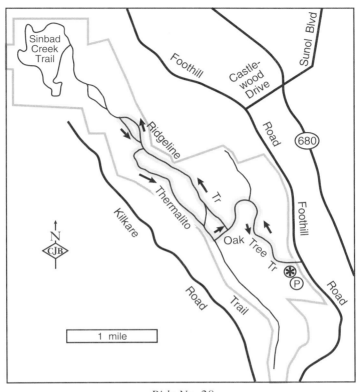

Ride No. 28

Ridgeline Trail in Pleasanton Ridge Regional Park.

29 Newark
Coyote Hills Regional Park

Region: *East Bay*
Difficulty Rating: *Easy*
Skill Level: *Beginner*
Elevation Gain: *100 feet*

Total Distance: *15 miles*
Off-Road Distance: *15 miles*
Riding Time: *2 hours*
Total Calories: *300*

About the Ride

Home to Ohlone Indians for over 2,000 years, Coyote Hills is today a unique place to experience the wetlands of San Francisco Bay. Crossed with a network of hiking and biking trails, the grassy hillsides of the park stand out against the flat low-lying land all around. The marshes and mudflats along the coastline are home to the many insects and marine animals, which serve as the food supply for the wide variety of birds frequently seen in the park.

This route takes you into the park and immediately heads south along the shore of the bay toward the San Francisco Bay National Wildlife Refuge, where you can get off your bike, explore the wetlands, and tour the informative visitor center there. Back at Coyote Hills, the route leads north along Bayview Trail and then out into the bay along the Alameda Creek Regional Trail. Riding along the Shoreline Trail past the salt ponds, you can experience the magnificence of the bay while you view the Dumbarton Bridge in the distance. The return to the park puts you again on the Bayview Trail as it follows the shoreline. Through the marshes and past the Indian Mound Archaeological Site, you return to the parking lot.

The ride is very flat along mostly paved trails, except for some stretches on loose gravel.

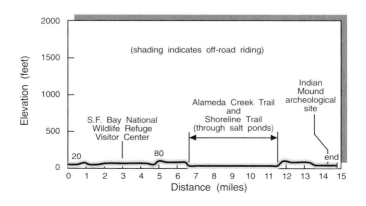

Starting Point

Start the ride at the parking lot at the entrance to Coyote Hills Regional Park. To get there, take Highway 880 to Newark and get off at the exit for Highway 84. Head west on Highway 84, toward the Dumbarton Bridge and exit at Ardenwood Boulevard. Proceed north on Ardenwood Boulevard, turn left onto Paseo Padre Parkway, right onto Patterson Ranch Road, and follow this road into Coyote Hills Park.

Mile Markers

0.0 Proceed WEST out of the parking area into Coyote Hills Regional Park on the paved trail that runs parallel to the roadway.

0.4 Turn LEFT onto Bayview Trail and cross the road.

0.9 Bear LEFT to stay on paved trail.

1.1 Bear RIGHT toward Shoreline Trail and Apay Way.

1.2 Turn LEFT onto San Francisco Bay Trail (Apay Way) – dirt trail.

2.6 Cross Highway 84 on bridge overpass.

3.0 San Francisco Bay National Wildlife Refuge visitor center. Be sure to stop for a visit and a walk through the wetlands. When you are finished, return the way you came.

4.8 Turn LEFT back onto paved Bayview Trail.

6.5 Turn LEFT toward Alameda Creek and then turn LEFT again onto Alameda Creek Regional Trail, heading west toward the bay — unpaved trail.

8.7 Begin Shoreline Trail in S.F. Bay National Wildlife Refuge. Dumbarton Bridge is visible ahead.

9.6 Continue STRAIGHT toward Coyote Hills. Shoreline Trail turns to the right at this point.

11.5 Turn LEFT onto paved Bayview Trail back in Coyote Hills Regional Park.

13.2 Continue STRAIGHT on Bayview Trail at the point where Alameda Creek Trail access is to the left.

13.6 Turn LEFT onto Lizard Rock Trail toward Chochenyo Trail.

13.8 Turn LEFT onto unmarked trail.

14.0 Turn RIGHT onto unmarked trail through the marsh and then turn LEFT onto Chochenyo Trail toward Indian Mound.

14.3 Turn RIGHT to go around the Indian Mound archaeological site — closed to the public.

14.4 Bear RIGHT at the far end of the site.

14.8 Back at the parking lot.

Further Information

East Bay Regional Park District: (510) 531-9300

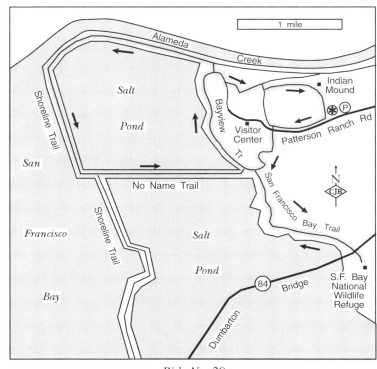

Ride No. 29

The salt ponds of Coyote Hills Park.

30   Livermore
Morgan Territory

Region: *East Bay*
Difficulty Rating: *Easy*
Skill Level: *Easy*
Elevation Gain: *600 feet*

Total Distance: *7 miles*
Off-Road Distance: *7 miles*
Riding Time: *1-2 hours*
Total Calories: *400*

About the Ride

Just north of Livermore is a quiet country road leading toward Clayton along the eastern slope of Mount Diablo. Morgan Territory Road is about as remote as you can get, considering how close to the population centers of the Bay Area it is.

Morgan Territory Regional Preserve, located at the top of the hill on Morgan Territory Road, is tiny in comparison to nearby Mount Diablo State Park. Its small size and relative obscurity offer the mountain biker a chance to experience classic East Bay trails without the crowds, which sometimes exist at Mount Diablo.

This ride will lead you on a tour completely through Morgan Territory. Since the route starts at the main park entrance at a 1,900-foot elevation, it offers the beginner mountain biker a chance to experience high country panoramas without having to undertake the massive climbs to get there. Proceeding initially along the wide and relatively flat fire trails, Volvon Trail and Blue Oak Trail, it suddenly takes you steeply downhill along Valley View Trail. Aptly named, Valley View Trail offers stunning vistas east into the San Joaquin Valley and toward Discovery Bay. The climb back up has several short steep sections, but is generally not very difficult. The Volvon Loop Trail leads back to Volvon Trail for the return to the starting point.

Watch for equestrians and always slow down when you see them, as horses can sometimes spook quite easily. The summers are quite hot in the East Bay, so be sure to bring along plenty of water.

Starting Point

Start the ride at the main entrance to Morgan Territory Regional Preserve. To get there, take Highway 580 to Livermore and get off at North Livermore Avenue. Follow North Livermore Avenue 4 miles north, away from Livermore, and then turn right onto Morgan Territory Road. The Preserve is located on top of the hill about 6 miles up the road.

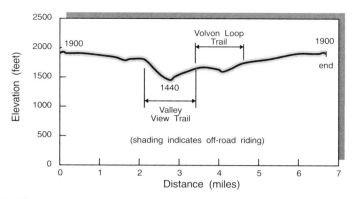

Mile Markers

0.0 Proceed into the park along Volvon Trail.

0.3 Continue along Volvon Trail as it merges with a wide fire road coming in from right side.

0.6 Turn LEFT to stay on Volvon Trail (straight ahead has no outlet.) Just after this turn, bear RIGHT onto Blue Oak Trail.

1.2 Bear LEFT to stay on Blue Oak Trail (Manzanita Trail branches to right.)

1.4 Bear RIGHT to stay on Blue Oak Trail (Hummingbird Trail branches to left.)

2.0 Turn RIGHT onto Volvon Trail.

2.1 Continue through gate and turn RIGHT immediately onto Valley View Trail. Prepare for steep downhill section.

2.8 Views of the Central Valley.

3.2 Continue STRAIGHT toward Volvon Loop Trail.

3.3 Turn RIGHT onto Volvon Loop Trail.

4.0 Turn LEFT to stay on Volvon Loop Trail (Eagle Trail branches to right.)

4.6 Continue STRAIGHT through the livestock gate (Valley View Trail is on the left.)

5.3 Turn RIGHT to stay on Volvon Trail (Hummingbird Trail is on left.)

6.0 Turn RIGHT to stay on Volvon Trail (Blue Oak Trail on the left.) From here, return back the way you came.

6.7 End of the ride at the parking lot.

Further Information

East Bay Regional Park District: (510) 531-9300

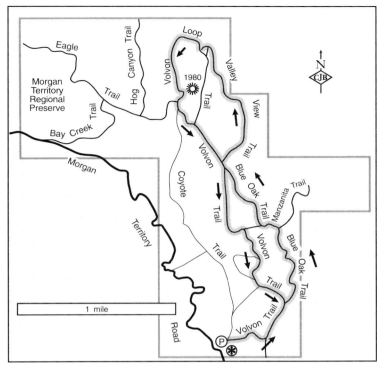

Ride No. 30

Valley View Trail in Morgan Territory.

31 Sunol
Sunol-Ohlone Regional Wilderness

Region: *East Bay*
Difficulty Rating: *Difficult*
Skill Level: *Intermediate*
Elevation Gain: *2000 feet*

Total Distance: *10 miles*
Off-Road Distance: *9 miles*
Riding Time: *3 hours*
Total Calories: *1100*

About the Ride

Several hundred years ago, Ohlone Indians lived and prospered in a small valley in the East Bay, somewhat east of what is today the town of Sunol. In its more recent past, the area was used extensively for cattle ranching. Today, the Sunol-Ohlone Regional Wilderness, administered by the East Bay Regional Parks District, is open to the general public for recreational uses. While the land is still used by local ranchers for cattle grazing, its primary function is to offer a wealth of diverse outdoor activities, like camping, backpacking, picnicking, hiking, horseback riding, and, of course, mountain biking. Little-known outside of the immediate East Bay region, the Sunol Wilderness contains many miles of trails over rugged terrain. Views of the nearby Calaveras Reservoir reward those hardy souls with the energy to climb to the upper trails within the park.

This ride will take you from the park headquarters along a level fire road toward "Little Yosemite," a picturesque camping area at the east end of the park. Before reaching the campground, the route turns and leads up a fairly steep trail toward the Cerro Este Overlook, the high spot on the ride. Eagle View Trail and Cave Rocks Trail lead along the ridge and then down to High Valley, where an old barn sits, along with some shaded picnic tables. Another climb up Vista Grande Road will take you to the paved Welch Creek Road and a fast descent to the trailhead for Flag Hill Road. Flag Hill Road will return you to High Valley Barn and then down the hill back to park headquarters along Hayfield Road.

While the terrain is quite steep in places, the trails are wide. Since they are not always clearly marked, riders will need to carefully note the directions in order to follow the route correctly. It is common to come across grazing cattle in the park, but they are normally quite passive.

Starting Point

Start the ride at the main parking area for Sunol Regional Wilderness. To get there, take Highway 680 toward Sunol and get off at

Calaveras Road. Be sure that you take the right exit, as there is also a Calaveras *Boulevard* in Milpitas. Follow Calaveras Road for 4 miles and then turn left on Geary Road. The park is 2 miles in on Geary Road.

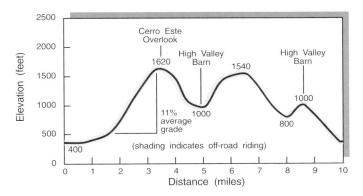

Mile Markers

0.0 Proceed into the park on the paved road, heading toward Little Yosemite.

0.5 Continue past gate, cross over a bridge and follow a wide fire road, Camp Ohlone Road.

1.6 Turn LEFT onto Cerro Este Road and begin steep climbing.

2.6 Continue STRAIGHT on Cerro Este Road, as McCorkle Trail merges in from the left.

3.0 Continue STRAIGHT on Cerro Este Road, as McCorkle Trail branches off to the right.

3.4 Turn LEFT onto Eagle View Trail. Cerro Este Overlook is on the left side with expansive views of Calaveras Reservoir to the south.

4.0 Continue STRAIGHT on Cave Rocks Road, as Eagle View Trail branches off to the right.

4.8 Just after the High Valley Barn, bear RIGHT to stay on Cave Rocks Road.

5.1 Turn RIGHT onto Vista Grande Road toward upper Welch Creek Road.

6.2 Turn LEFT onto Eagle View Trail as Vista Grande Road continues straight ahead.

6.6 Turn LEFT onto paved Welch Creek Road and begin descent.

7.4 Cross cattle guard.

7.9 Turn LEFT onto unmarked Flag Hill Road.

8.4 Continue STRAIGHT onto Cave Rocks Road at the junction with Vista Grande Road on the left.

8.6 Bear RIGHT at the High Valley Barn onto Hayfield Road and begin steep descent toward the park headquarters.

9.9 Turn RIGHT at the end of Hayfield Road and then turn LEFT immediately to cross the stream.

10.0 End of the ride back at the parking area.

Further Information

East Bay Regional Park District: (510) 531-9300

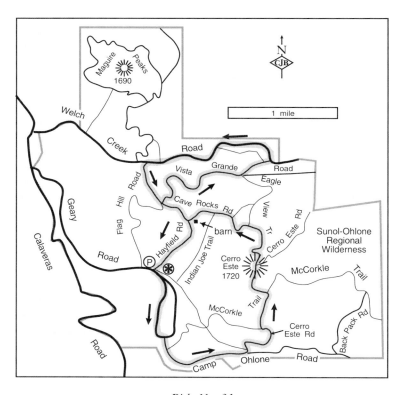

Ride No. 31

32 Lafayette
Briones Regional Park

Region: *East Bay*
Difficulty Rating: *Difficult*
Skill Level: *Intermediate*
Elevation Gain: *1700 feet*

Total Distance: *10 miles*
Off-Road Distance: *10 miles*
Riding Time: *2-3 hours*
Total Calories: *1000*

About the Ride

In the early 1800s, the land in what is today Briones Regional Park was settled by Felipe Briones. After passing through the hands of successive owners, the property was eventually acquired as part of the larger East Bay watershed, and later still, was transferred to the East Bay Regional Park District for use as recreational open space for residents. Today, the 5,303 acres serve the needs of equestrians, hikers, and cyclists.

This ride consists of a general tour of Briones Park, following the crests high above and around the park whenever possible. Stunning views of the distant countryside in all directions add to the grandeur of this strenuous ride. Grass and oak-covered slopes, heavily forested canyons and an occasional meadow give the cyclist a general flavor of the park and add to the temptation to further explore the many other trails in a later visit.

After passing through a small meadow at the beginning of the ride, the route climbs very steeply along Crescent Ridge Trail. Views from Briones Crest Trail and Briones Peak (1,400-foot elevation) are followed by a gradual descent to the far entrance of the park. After a short stretch on a paved section along Briones Road, Pine Tree Trail leads to Toyon Canyon Trail and another steep climb to Mott Peak. The steep descent on Black Oak Trail leads to another meadow and the return along Old Briones Road to the parking area.

The route follows wide fire trails across hills that are quite steep in places. Trails are well-marked and detailed maps are usually available at the park entrance.

Starting Point

Start the ride at the parking lot inside the Bear Creek Road entrance to Briones Regional Park. To get there, take the Pleasant Hill Road exit off Highway 24 in Lafayette. Go south on Pleasant Hill Road and immediately turn right onto Mt. Diablo Boulevard. Follow Mt. Diablo Boulevard for about 1.5 miles and turn right onto Happy Valley Road.

After about 4 miles, at the end of Happy Valley Road, turn right onto Bear Creek Road and look for the entrance to Briones Regional Park on the right side.

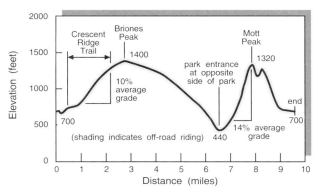

Mile Markers

0.0 Proceed out of the parking area into Briones Park on Old Briones Road Trail.

0.1 Continue past the gate and then turn RIGHT onto Homestead Valley Trail.

0.4 Continue past the gate, through the meadow, and then turn LEFT onto Crescent Ridge Trail.

0.9 Archery Range on right side, then begin steep climb.

1.7 Bear RIGHT to stay on Crescent Ridge Trail.

2.2 Continue past gate, then turn LEFT onto Briones Crest Trail.

2.7 Bear LEFT to stay on Briones Crest Trail (Table Top Trail intersection on the right).

4.2 Turn RIGHT onto Old Briones Road Trail.

4.7 Bear LEFT to stay on Old Briones Road Trail (Spengler Trail on right).

5.4 Continue past gate onto paved road.

5.8 Turn LEFT onto Pine Tree Trail at the gate on left side of road.

6.2 Turn LEFT onto Toyon Canyon Trail.

7.0 Bear LEFT onto Lagoon Trail.

7.6 Turn RIGHT onto Mott Peak Trail.

7.8 Bear LEFT to stay on Mott Peak Trail.

8.1 Turn LEFT onto Black Oak Trail.

8.9 Turn RIGHT onto Old Briones Road Trail.

9.4 Continue past gate, back to the start point.

Further Information

East Bay Regional Park District: (510) 531-9300

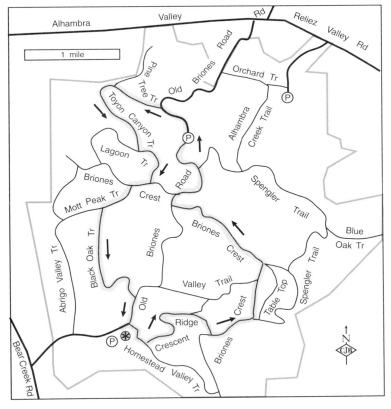

Ride No. 32

33 Berkeley
Tilden and Wildcat Canyon

Region: *East Bay*	**Total Distance:** *17 miles*
Difficulty Rating: *Moderate*	**Off-Road Distance:** *16 miles*
Skill Level: *Intermediate*	**Riding Time:** *2-3 hours*
Elevation Gain: *1700 feet*	**Total Calories:** *1200*

About the Ride

Tilden and Wildcat Canyon Regional Parks, located adjacent to each other in the Berkeley Hills, encompass over 4,000 acres of forests with trails for cycling, hiking, and equestrian use. In addition, Tilden Park includes a golf course, botanical garden, steam trains, pony rides, merry-go-round, nature area, and Lake Anza. Weekends find the parks fully utilized as the residents of the surrounding areas come here to relax and to enjoy the natural beauty of the place.

The first part of the ride consists of a short 4-mile loop through the southern section of Tilden Park. This section includes a fairly steep 500-foot climb, less ambitious riders may want to avoid it and begin the ride at the start of the long loop at the 3.9-mile mark.

The long loop leads through the northern section of Tilden Park and includes a tour of Wildcat Canyon, as well. The first 4 miles follow a paved section of trail on Chester Nimitz Way, named for the famous World War II admiral. From this relatively flat section at the top of the hills, there are stunning views of the surrounding areas in both directions. At the end of the paved trail, the route follows fire roads as it continues along the crest of the hills and then leads down a steep trail into Wildcat Canyon. After riding through the canyon in the lower elevations, the route leads past serene Jewel Lake and then follows a forested trail as it takes you back to Inspiration Point.

The trails in Tilden and Wildcat Canyon Regional Parks are wide fire roads and are steep and somewhat rough in some sections.

Starting Point

Start the ride at Inspiration Point on Wildcat Canyon Road. To get there from the east, take Highway 24 to the Orinda exit and proceed north on Camino Pablo. Turn left onto Wildcat Canyon Road and follow it about 2.5 miles to Inspiration Point, on the right side.

From the west, take Ashby Avenue, in Berkeley, east to Claremont Avenue. Follow Claremont Avenue up into the Berkeley Hills and turn left onto Grizzly Peak Boulevard. Turn right onto South Park Drive and right again onto Wildcat Canyon Road. After about 1.5 miles on Wildcat Canyon Road, Inspiration Point will be on the left side.

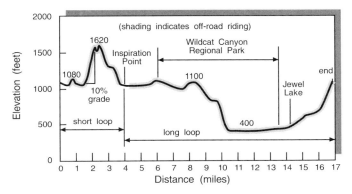

Mile Markers

0.0 Proceed out of the parking lot and turn RIGHT onto Wildcat Canyon Road.

0.4 Turn LEFT into Quarry Picnic Area and follow signs for the trail, just past the picnic tables.

0.7 Bear RIGHT to stay on Quarry Trail.

1.5 Continue STRAIGHT to get on Big Springs Trail and proceed past the parking lot to continue on the trail at the far side.

2.0 Turn LEFT onto Seaview Trail along the ridge.

3.3 Big Springs Trail intersection on the left side.

3.7 Turn RIGHT onto Wildcat Canyon Road at the end of the trail.

3.9 Back at Inspiration Point. Begin the long loop by proceeding into Tilden Park through the gate onto Nimitz Way.

5.8 Enter Wildcat Canyon Park at cattle guard.

6.1 Conlon Trail intersection on the left side.

8.0 Veer LEFT onto gravel trail and continue past gate.

8.2 Turn LEFT onto Mezue Trail and then RIGHT onto San Pablo Ridge Trail.

9.4 Bear LEFT onto Belgum Trail.

9.5 Clark Boas Trail intersection on right side.

10.3 Continue STRAIGHT at the gate and then turn LEFT onto the unimproved paved road toward Tilden Nature Area.

11.1 Turn RIGHT off road and continue on paved section to gravel trail just ahead.

13.5 Enter Tilden Nature Area.

14.3 Bear LEFT just past Jewel Lake onto Loop Trail.

14.8 Bear RIGHT to stay on Loop Trail.

15.1 Turn LEFT to stay on Loop Trail and continue past gate onto paved road.

15.3 Turn LEFT at the Lone Oak Picnic Ground to get on fire trail and then bear RIGHT onto Wildcat Gorge Trail.

16.1 Turn LEFT onto Curran Trail.

16.6 Bear RIGHT at Meadow Canyon Trail intersection on the left.

16.8 Back at Inspiration Point.

Further Information

East Bay Regional Park District: (510) 531-9300

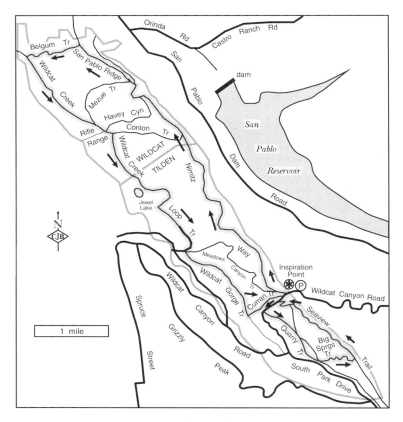

Ride No. 33

Facing page photo:
Tranquil Jewel Lake in Tilden Regional Park.

34 Danville
Mount Diablo State Park

Region: *East Bay*
Difficulty Rating: *Difficult*
Skill Level: *Intermediate*
Elevation Gain: *1800 feet*

Total Distance: *9 miles*
Off-Road Distance: *8 miles*
Riding Time: *2 hours*
Total Calories: *1100*

About the Ride

Dominating the landscape in the East Bay, Mount Diablo towers to a height of 3,849 feet and can be seen from nearly anywhere in the Bay Area. Easily the largest single park in the East Bay, Mount Diablo State Park offers its visitors many miles of trails for hiking, cycling, and horseback riding. This ride is located in the western part of the park and is easily accessible from Alamo and Danville. It is ideal as an introduction to the park, by virtue of the wide variety of terrain and geology along the way and with the stunning views of the distant summit above and the population centers below.

Starting at the historic Macedo Ranch Staging Area, the trail first leads uphill through active pasture land, where it is common to encounter grazing cattle up close. After this short climb, the route then leads down into Pine Canyon and follows along Pine Creek. The climb out of the canyon to Barbecue Terrace is a long and steep one, as the trail passes through grassy hillsides and leads to panoramic views at the top. A short downhill stretch along the paved main road through the park leads to the trailhead for the return leg of the tour along Summit Trail and Wall Point Road. Wall Point Road is a fire road that first leads through the large sandstone formations of Rock City and then along a narrow ridge with dramatic drop-offs in both directions. From the ridge, Danville and Walnut Creek are visible to the west and the Mount Diablo Summit can be seen in the east. Also to the east, you can look down into Pine Canyon and see where the earlier part of the ride took place. A long and sometimes steep descent takes you back to the starting point at Macedo Ranch.

The route follows wide fire roads, often quite steep, with loose gravel in some places. Trails are not always marked, so be sure to follow the route directions very carefully. Poison oak is very common along the trails, so avoid contact with anything.

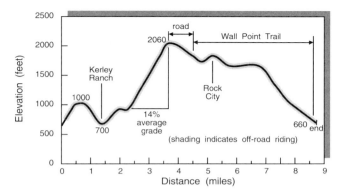

Starting Point

Start the ride in Danville, at the end of Green Valley Road. To get there, take the Stone Valley Road exit from Highway 680 and follow Stone Valley Road east about three miles to Green Valley Road. Turn left onto Green Valley Road, follow it to its end, and park at the Macedo Ranch Staging Area.

Mile Markers

0.0   Proceed EAST on the Wall Point Road fire trail, located on the right side of the parking area.

0.3   Bear RIGHT to stay on Wall Point Road.

0.8   Turn LEFT onto Pine Canyon Trail. Wall Point Road continues to the right.

1.3   Go past livestock gate and turn RIGHT onto Stage Road at Kerley Ranch.

1.7   Continue STRAIGHT toward Barbecue Terrace. Buckeye Trail goes to the left.

3.3   Continue past gate and turn RIGHT onto paved service road.

3.6   Turn RIGHT onto South Gate Road, the main road in the park.

4.5   Turn RIGHT onto Summit Trail toward Rock City. Trailhead is in a small turnout on the right side of the road and is easy to miss.

4.8   Trail ends back at the main road — turn RIGHT onto Wall Point Road fire road.

7.5   Bear RIGHT to stay on Wall Point Road. Emmons Canyon Road intersection on the left side.

7.9   Bear LEFT to stay on Wall Point Road toward Macedo Ranch. Pine Canyon Trail is on right side.

8.7   Back at the Macedo Ranch parking area.

Further Information

Mount Diablo State Park: (510) 837-2525

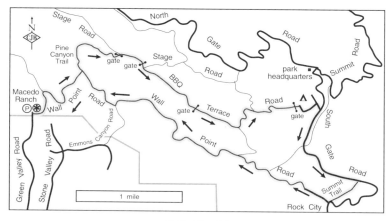

Ride No. 34

The rolling hills of Mt. Diablo.

35 Clayton
Mt. Diablo State Park – Mitchell Canyon

Region: *East Bay*
Difficulty Rating: *Difficult*
Skill Level: *Advanced*
Elevation Gain: *1900 feet*

Total Distance: *9 miles*
Off-Road Distance: *9 miles*
Riding Time: *2 hours*
Total Calories: *1100*

About the Ride

Rising to an elevation of 3,849 feet, Mount Diablo is a dominating presence in the East Bay as it towers over the surrounding hills and flatlands. Trails and fire roads within Mt. Diablo State Park provide hikers, equestrians, and mountain bikers innumerable routes from which to choose.

The eastern side of the park, near the town of Clayton, serves as the venue for this ride. Somewhat isolated from the population centers of the larger cities on the west side of the mountain, its trails often have less traffic on them.

The Mitchell Canyon entrance to the park is the starting point of the ride. The route begins with a very slight uphill grade leading through Mitchell Canyon. Mountainsides on each side of the trail offer a feeling of protection and tranquility as you casually warm up your legs through this section. At the end of the canyon, about 2 miles into the ride, the trail leads upward on a sharply steeper grade. Expect to use your lowest gears as you climb steadily for about 1.5 miles on a 14% slope. At Deer Flat, there is a major trail junction and a small downhill section before an even steeper climb. The descent back down the mountain is also quite steep and may be easier if you lower your seat before you head down. The views toward Clayton are breathtaking on this side of the hill. Once at the bottom, there is a final stretch back to the starting point across about one mile of relatively flat grassland.

While the fire roads are wide and generally quite smooth, the extreme steepness of both the uphill and downhill grades make this ride very challenging. It is usually quite dry in the summer months, so be sure to bring along adequate water.

Starting Point

Start the ride at the Mitchell Canyon entrance to Mount Diablo State Park, located just south of Clayton. Get there by taking either Highway 680 or Highway 24 to Walnut Creek. Get off Highway 680 at Ygnacio Valley Road and follow it east through Walnut Creek until you reach

Clayton. Turn right (heading south) on Clayton Road for about 1.5 miles and then turn right onto Mitchell Canyon Road. At the end of the road is the park entrance with restrooms and parking.

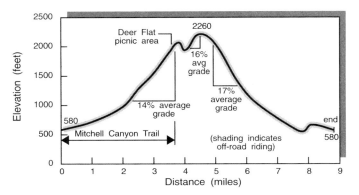

Mile Markers

0.0 Proceed from parking area into the park on Mitchell Canyon Trail along a gentle upward grade.

1.0 Fire road intersection on right side.

2.0 Begin steep climb.

3.6 Picnic tables on right side (Deer Flat).

3.8 Bear LEFT onto Prospector's Gap Fire Road toward North Peak.

4.4 High point — 2,260-foot elevation.

4.5 Eagle Peak Trail intersection on left side.

4.9 Turn LEFT on Meridian Ridge Trail toward Donner Canyon Trail — very steep descent.

5.7 Meridian Point Trail intersection on left side.

6.3 Turn LEFT on Donner Canyon Trail toward Regency Gate.

7.6 Unmarked fire road intersection on right side, then turn LEFT on another unmarked fire road over a grass-covered hill (Regency Gate is straight ahead).

7.8 Trail intersection on the right side, then another on the left. Continue STRAIGHT ahead.

8.1 Continue STRAIGHT ahead at 4-way trail intersection and follow parallel to wood fence ahead on the right side of the trail.

8.7 Continue STRAIGHT ahead at another 4-way trail intersection into parking lot just ahead.

8.8 End of the ride, back at the parking area.

Further Information

Mount Diablo State Park: (510) 837-2525

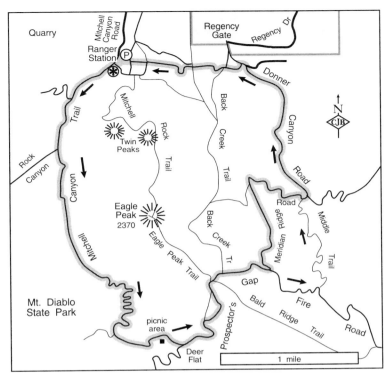

Ride No. 35

Mitchell Canyon in Mt. Diablo State Park.

The North Bay

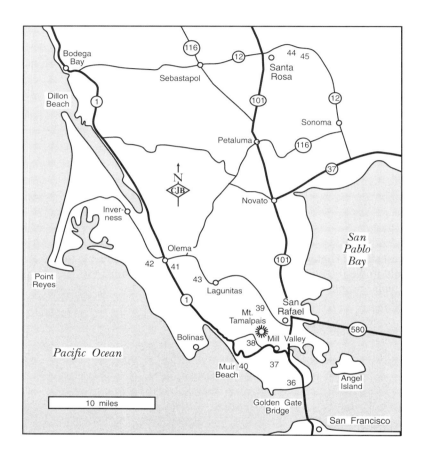

36 San Francisco

Golden Gate Bridge and Marin Headlands

Region: *North Bay*	**Total Distance:** *24 miles*
Difficulty Rating: *Difficult*	**Off-Road Distance:** *10 miles*
Skill Level: *Intermediate*	**Riding Time:** *4 hours*
Elevation Gain: *2800 feet*	**Total Calories:** *1500*

About the Ride

During World War II, the nation's defenses included major anti-aircraft installations along the Pacific Coast to protect against attack from foreign aircraft. Some remnants of those times are present today just north of San Francisco across the Golden Gate Bridge.

The Golden Gate National Recreation Area includes what is more commonly called the Marin Headlands. These hills, easily seen on the west side of Highway 101, across the bridge from the city, are home not only to the ruined battlements, but also to the many trails and fire roads which meander across the hills and through the canyons of this public-use land. Long a favorite of San Francisco hikers and equestrians, the Marin Headlands became a playground for bicyclists when the mountain bike came on the scene a few years back.

This ride begins on the San Francisco side of the Golden Gate Bridge. After crossing the bridge, the route takes you up the main paved road toward the bunkers at the top and then down the other side to Fort Cronkhite and Rodeo Beach. After a short stop at the beach, you hit the trails, climb over a hill on fire roads, and then descend into Tennessee Valley, a major jumping-off point for visitors to the area. Another climb on Marinchello Trail leads to panoramic views toward Sausalito, Angel Island, and Richardson Bay, before dropping down yet again near Fort Cronkhite. One final climb takes you back over a hill and down to the bridge for your return to where you started.

The trails are wide, generally smooth, and not terribly steep. There are four distinct climbs along the route, however, and that's what makes the ride rather strenuous.

Starting Point

Start the ride at the San Francisco side of the Golden Gate Bridge, on Merchant Road very near to the toll booth. To get there, take Highway 101 as if you were going to go north across the bridge. Get off at the vista point at the toll booth, go through the parking lot and turn right on Lincoln Boulevard. Cross under the bridge approach road, turn right on Merchant Road, and park near the bridge toll booth.

If you are coming from the North Bay, begin the ride at the north side of the bridge and pick it up at the 2.2 mile marker point.

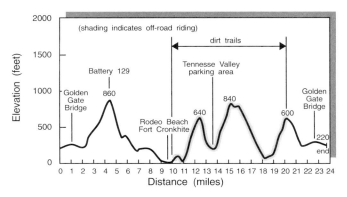

Mile Markers

0.0 Proceed through tunnel under bridge roadway and head NORTH across Golden Gate Bridge.

2.2 Turn LEFT onto Conzelman Road on the north side of the bridge.

3.6 Bear LEFT to stay on Conzelman Road at the intersection with McCullogh Road on the right side.

4.2 Battery 129 on the right side — bunkers and tunnels dating from World War II.

6.5 Continue STRAIGHT at the intersection toward Point Bonita.

6.9 Fort Barry — turn LEFT on the main road toward lighthouse.

7.0 Point Bonita lighthouse on the left — continue STRAIGHT.

7.3 End of the road with views of Rodeo Beach and Fort Cronkhite — turn around and return the way you came.

8.8 Visitor Center on the left.

8.9 Turn LEFT toward Rodeo Beach.

9.3 Bear LEFT toward the beach.

9.8 Rodeo Beach — turn around and return the way you came.

10.5 Just past last building of Fort Cronkhite on the left, turn LEFT off the main road and get on Miwok Trail.

10.8 Continue STRAIGHT at intersection with Rodeo Valley Trail on the right.

11.0 Continue STRAIGHT at intersection with Bobcat Trail on the right.

12.4 Turn LEFT onto Old Springs Trail.

Bay Area Mountain Bike Trails

13.6 Continue through the stable area toward parking lot.

13.8 Turn RIGHT onto Marinchello Trail just after Miwok Trail intersection.

15.3 Bear LEFT to get on Bobcat Trail.

16.0 Bear RIGHT to stay on Bobcat Trail.

18.1 Turn LEFT onto Rodeo Valley Trail.

18.3 Bear RIGHT at trail split.

18.5 Cross small bridge and then turn LEFT onto paved road.

18.7 Cross main road and get on trail on the far side. Continue through clearing and turn LEFT onto main trail.

19.0 Continue past gate onto Coastal Trail.

20.3 Exit past gate and turn LEFT onto Conzelman Road.

21.4 Turn RIGHT onto road leading back toward bridge and cross bridge back to San Francisco.

23.7 End of the ride, back at the start point.

Further Information

Golden Gate National Recreation Area
Marin Headlands Ranger Station: (415) 561-7612
Tennessee Valley Ranger Station: (415) 383-7717

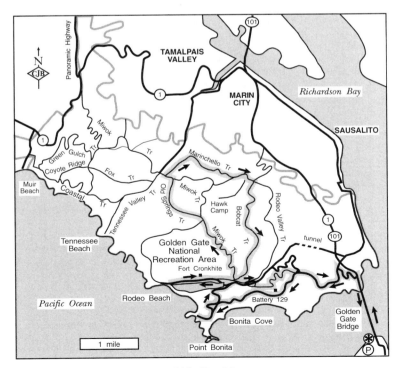

Ride No. 36

37　Mill Valley
Marin Headlands — Tennessee Valley and Muir Beach Loop

Region: *North Bay*
Difficulty Rating: *Moderate*
Skill Level: *Intermediate*
Elevation Gain: *1700 feet*

Total Distance: *11 miles*
Off-Road Distance: *9 miles*
Riding Time: *2 hours*
Total Calories: *1000*

About the Ride

Just across the Golden Gate Bridge from San Francisco lies the Marin Headlands, a part of the Golden Gate National recreation Area (GGNRA). Encircled by many miles of trails and fire roads, the Marin Headlands has long been a popular hiking and horseback riding area for residents of San Francisco and of Marin County. While the single-track trails are mostly off-limits to mountain bike enthusiasts, the fire roads are not and offer some of the most spectacular scenery in the entire Bay Area.

This ride consists of a loop around the northern part of the Headlands, beginning at the Tennessee Valley parking area, a popular starting point for all park users. Weekends usually find the Tennessee Valley parking lot full, so it may be necessary to park along Tennessee Valley Road and to ride in.

The route follows the heavily used Tennessee Valley Trail, paved and flat and an easy warm-up, from the parking lot all the way to the beach. From there, Coastal Trail will get your heart rate up as it leads you to the top of the ridge. Coyote Ridge Trail will then take you along a steep downhill section to Muir Beach. Be sure to stop and savor the fabulous vistas as you approach Muir Beach, where there are picnic tables and restrooms.

A two-mile stretch on busy Highway 1 is necessary to connect with the return on Miwok Trail. (If you prefer to avoid Highway 1, you can always return back the way you came, but Miwok Trail is quite spectacular and not to be missed.) Highway 1 will take you up a hill to the connection with Miwok Trail. Miwok Trail follows along the ridge line and then drops steeply down back into Tennessee Valley at the end. The views of Sausalito and Richardson Bay from the top are simply sensational as you ride along the spine of the mountains.

There is some steep terrain throughout the ride, but the climbs are not horrendous. The highest point in the ride is only about 900 feet above sea level. The most difficult riding is actually along each of the two downhill stretches. They are steep and require great caution.

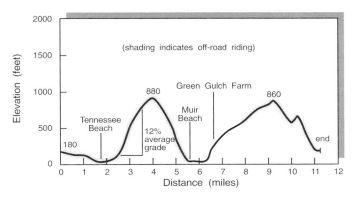

Starting Point

Start the ride at the Tennessee Valley parking lot for Marin Headlands. Get there by taking Highway 101 to southern Marin County. Get off at the exit for Highway 1 toward Stinson beach. Follow Highway 1 for about 1 mile and look for Tennessee Valley Road on the left side. The parking lot is located about 2 miles in.

Mile Markers

0.0 Proceed WEST on Tennessee Valley Trail, heading toward the beach.

0.6 Begin dirt trail.

1.2 Continue STRAIGHT at intersection with Coastal Trail on the right side.

1.8 Tennessee Beach — return the way you came.

2.4 Turn LEFT onto Coastal Trail and begin climbing.

3.1 Turn RIGHT to head toward Coyote Ridge Trail.

3.9 Turn LEFT onto Coyote Ridge Trail (Fox Trail is on the right) and then continue STRAIGHT on Coyote Ridge Trail toward Muir Beach (Coyote Ridge Trail also branches to the right.) Prepare for steep descent.

5.3 Continue STRAIGHT at intersection with Green Gulch Trail on the right side.

5.4 Just after Green Gulch Trail intersection, follow trail as it turns to the RIGHT to head toward the road.

5.7 Turn RIGHT onto the unmarked road and head for Highway 1. (If you wish to visit Muir Beach, turn left here and then come back when you are done.)

5.8 Turn RIGHT onto Highway 1. This road can be very busy with car traffic and has no shoulder, so be very careful and stay all the way to the right.

6.4 Zen Center — Green Gulch Farm on the right side.

7.8 At the top of the grade, turn RIGHT onto well-marked Miwok Trail.

9.4 Turn LEFT to stay on Miwok Trail as Coyote Ridge Trail intersects on the right side.

10.0 Turn RIGHT to Stay on Miwok Trail (park exit is on the left side.)

10.2 Trail intersection on the right side, then turn RIGHT to stay on Miwok Trail toward Tennessee Valley.

10.6 Begin single-track section — steep and narrow descent.

11.2 End of the ride back at parking area.

Further Information

Golden Gate National Recreation Area

Marin Headlands Ranger Station: (415) 561-7612
Tennessee Valley Ranger Station: (415) 383-7717

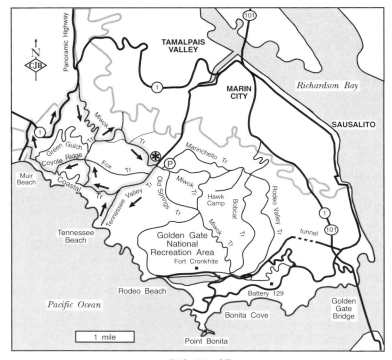

Ride No. 37

38   Mill Valley
Mt. Tamalpais East Peak Loop

Region: *North Bay*	**Total Distance:** *12 miles*
Difficulty Rating: *Moderate*	**Off-Road Distance:** *12 miles*
Skill Level: *Intermediate*	**Riding Time:** *2-3 hours*
Elevation Gain: *1500 feet*	**Total Calories:** *900*

About the Ride

The mountain biking boom had its birth in the hills of Mt. Tamalpais State Park in Marin County. The all-terrain bike was first developed here by hiking and bicycling enthusiasts who saw the need for a rugged and durable bike, and who had the vision of what it would lead to. While moderately accessible on foot, the many trails around Mt. Tamalpais can be covered with relative ease on a bike.

This ride consists of a loop around Mt. Tamalpais East Peak, the highest point in the park, rising to an elevation of 2,570 feet. It follows the most popular of the trails in the park, used by hikers and equestrians, as well as mountain bikers, so it is important to be very careful and not to use excessive speed on the trails.

The ride begins at the parking lot at Mountain Home Inn, on Panoramic Highway near the picturesque town of Mill Valley. On weekends, the parking lot is usually full, so it may be necessary to park along the road somewhere and to bike to the starting point.

The route initially follows Gravity Car Grade, a generally flat fire road leading to the main loop. Hoo-Koo-E-Koo Road is a fire trail which winds along the ridge to connect with Indian Road and to Eldridge Grade for the main climb in the ride. Indian Road and Eldridge Grade are both fairly steep and can be a bit bumpy, but slow and steady riding will get you to the top. You can expect to see Lake Lagunitas and Bon Tempe Lake to the north along the top section of Eldridge Grade. Old Railroad Grade will take you down off the mountain, passing by historic West Point Inn, where you can stop for a snack and a refreshing lemonade on hot summer days. The return to the starting point is back the way you came along Gravity Car Grade.

The only steep and bumpy sections are uphill along Indian Road and Eldridge Grade — the downhills are quite modest and the trails are generally wide and smooth. Bicycle speed limits are 15 miles per hour within the park and are strictly enforced. Trail signs are not always clear — be sure to follow the route directions closely.

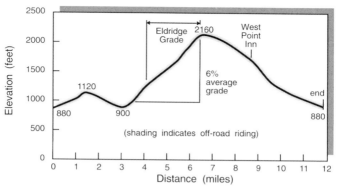

(shading indicates off-road riding)

Starting Point

Start the ride at the main parking lot on Panoramic Highway at Mountain Home Inn. To get there, take Highway 101 to southern Marin County and get off at the exit for Highway 1 and Stinson Beach. Follow Highway 1 (Shoreline Highway) for about 3 miles and turn right on Panoramic Highway. The parking lot and Mountain Home Inn are easy to find about 2-3 miles up the road.

Mile Markers

0.0 Proceed from the parking lot and cross the road onto the paved road on the other side. Bear right onto a dirt road into the Mt. Tamalpais Watershed area and continue past the gate into the park.

1.0 Bear LEFT at trail split onto Old Railroad Grade and continue STRAIGHT at the trail intersection on the right side shortly thereafter.

1.4 Turn RIGHT onto Hoo-Koo-E-Koo Road.

3.4 Turn LEFT onto Blithedale Ridge Road and then LEFT again onto Indian Road.

4.1 Turn LEFT onto Eldridge Grade and prepare for a bumpy and rocky ascent.

6.7 Trail ends at paved road. Turn RIGHT onto road and look for trailhead on far side of the road a short distance ahead. Proceed on this trail, Old Railroad Grade.

8.7 Historic West Point Inn on the left side. Snacks and beverages are available here. Continue past the inn on Old Railroad Grade.

9.5 Intersection with Hogback Road on the right side.

10.3 Intersection with Hoo-Koo-E-Koo Road on the left side.

10.7 Continue STRAIGHT at the trail intersection on the left and proceed toward Mountain Home.

11.8 End of the ride at the parking lot at Mountain Home Inn.

Further Information

Mt. Tamalpais Pantoll Ranger Station: (415) 388-2070
Marin Municipal Water District —
    Sky Oaks Ranger Station: (415) 459-5267

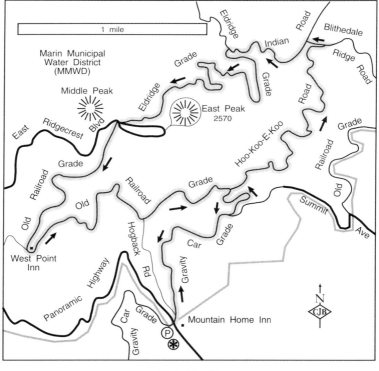

Ride No. 38

39 Ross
Mt. Tamalpais Watershed — Lakes Loop

Region: *North Bay*	**Total Distance:** *11 miles*
Difficulty Rating: *Moderate*	**Off-Road Distance:** *9 miles*
Skill Level: *Intermediate*	**Riding Time:** *2 hours*
Elevation Gain: *1100 feet*	**Total Calories:** *800*

About the Ride

The water for Marin County is provided by the lakes located in the Mt. Tamalpais Watershed. Administered by the Marin Municipal Water District (MMWD) and located just north of majestic Mt. Tamalpais, the lakes are ringed by a network of trails and fire roads which lead through the surrounding woodlands and across the rolling hills.

This ride passes by several of the lakes in the watershed. Starting at Greene Park near the town of Ross, the route leads up a fire road to Phoenix Lake, after which Shaver Grade climbs to the major Four Corners trail junction. Shaver Grade continues climbing past Four Corners, leading even higher to its end at Sky Oaks Road. A brief stretch on the road will take you to the trailhead for Bullfrog Road, a dirt trail toward Alpine Lake and Bon Tempe Lake. Back on Sky Oaks Road, the route will then take you directly past Bon Tempe Lake and to another trailhead leading toward quiet and pristine Lake Lagunitas. After circling the lake along the wooded shoreline, more fire trails lead you back to Phoenix Lake and the starting point of the ride.

The trails are all wide, not very steep and generally smooth. They are not well-marked and sometimes not even named, so it is important to follow the ride directions closely.

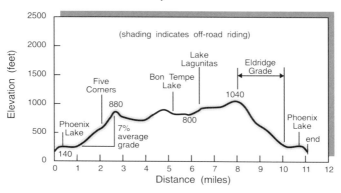

Starting Point

Start the ride at Natalie Coffin Greene Park in Ross. To get there, take Highway 101 to Marin County and get off at the exit for Sir Francis Drake Boulevard. Follow Sir Francis Drake Boulevard west about 3 miles to Ross and look for Lagunitas Road on the left side. Turn left on Lagunitas Road and follow it to the end where Greene Park is located.

Mile Markers

0.0   Proceed WEST out of parking lot along the paved road.

0.3   Continue STRAIGHT around the right side of Phoenix Lake.

1.0   At Phoenix Junction, bear RIGHT onto Shaver Grade.

2.1   At Five Corners, turn hard LEFT to continue uphill on Shaver Grade.

2.7   End of fire road — turn RIGHT onto the paved road.

3.0   Turn LEFT onto unmarked fire road at parking area on left side (Sky Oaks Ranger Station is just ahead on the right side.) Bear LEFT at trail split almost immediately.

3.9   Gate — continue STRAIGHT on gravel road.

4.0   Parking lot on right side with trail to Bon Tempe Dam.

4.5   Turn RIGHT onto the paved road.

5.2   Bon Tempe Lake on the right side.

5.7   Turn RIGHT at the "T" toward Lake Lagunitas.

5.9   Parking lot and picnic area — proceed on the trailhead on the right side of the parking area. This is Rock Springs-Lagunitas Road.

6.3   Lake Lagunitas on the left side.

6.4   Bear LEFT to continue around the lake. Rock Springs-Lagunitas Road branches off to the right.

7.3   Cross bridge and turn RIGHT at trail "T" onto unmarked fire road.

8.0   Turn LEFT onto Eldridge Grade and begin descent.

8.8   Continue STRAIGHT at trail junction on the right side.

9.3   Turn RIGHT at unmarked trail junction to continue on downhill on Eldridge Grade. This section is somewhat narrow and bumpy.

10.1   Back at Phoenix Junction, turn RIGHT onto Shaver Grade, heading toward Phoenix Lake.

10.4   Phoenix Lake on the right side.

11.1   End of the ride back at the parking area.

Further Information

Marin Municipal Water District —
Sky Oaks Ranger Station: (415) 459-5267

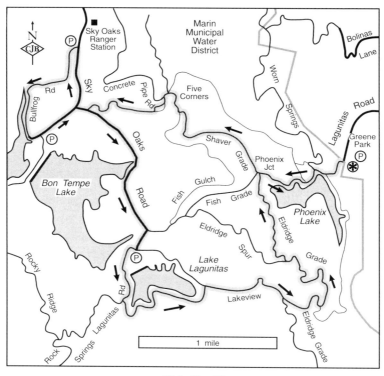

Ride No. 39

40 Muir Beach
Mt. Tamalpais and Muir Woods

Region: North Bay
Difficulty Rating: Moderate
Skill Level: Intermediate
Elevation Gain: 1300 feet

Total Distance: 9 miles
Off-Road Distance: 5 miles
Riding Time: 2 hours
Total Calories: 800

About the Ride

Just north of San Francisco lies one of the most impressive stands of ancient redwoods in the Bay Area. Muir Woods National Monument has long beckoned visitors with its giant trees and beautiful secluded trails. The density of the forest in Muir Woods contrasts sharply with the nearby Mt. Tamalpais State Park, characterized more by its wide open hillsides and rugged peaks. Whereas Mt. Tam (as it is called by the locals) has numerous fire roads open to mountain bikers, Muir Woods does not. Most of the park is off-limits to bikes, with the exception of Deer Park Fire Road.

This ride consists of a loop through both Mt. Tamalpais State Park and Muir Woods. The route starts at Muir Beach and initially leads north along Highway 1 for about 1.5 miles to reach the trailhead into Mt. Tamalpais. Coastal Trail is a wide fire road which climbs steeply along the ridge line. If you ride on a clear day, be sure to savor the impressive views of the coast behind you as you make the climb. At the top of the hill — called "Cardiac Hill" on the park trail maps — you will turn onto Deer Park Fire Road and descend along the southern border of Muir Woods. The flavor of the ride changes suddenly as you leave the open hillsides and wind your way down through a heavy forest. Deer Park Fire Road ends at Muir Woods Road, from which you have but a short 2-mile downhill stretch back to Muir Beach.

The trailhead for Coastal Trail is not obvious, so be sure to look carefully for it at the appropriate time. It is quite steep and may require all but the strongest riders to walk in some short sections.

Starting Point

Start the ride at Muir Beach, just off Highway 1. To get there, take Highway 1 north from San Francisco or south from northern Marin County. Look for the Pelican Inn at the corner of Muir Woods Road. Muir Beach is just down the road and has parking and restrooms.

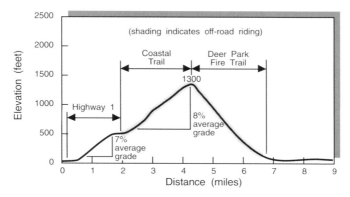

Mile Markers

0.0   Proceed out of Muir Beach parking area toward Highway 1.

0.2   Turn LEFT onto Highway 1.

0.4   Bear LEFT to stay on Highway 1 at Muir Woods Road intersection on right side. Begin to climb.

1.6   Turn RIGHT onto unmarked trail near the top of the grade. The trail runs parallel to the main road and will lead into Mt. Tamalpais State Park. There are several places to get on it along the road.

2.2   Continue past the gate into Mt. Tamalpais State Park and go STRAIGHT onto Coastal Trail. Prepare for steep climbing.

4.2   Turn RIGHT onto Deer Park Fire Road.

4.5   Dipsea Trail intersection on the right side.

6.7   End of the trail. Turn RIGHT onto Muir Woods Road.

8.6   Turn LEFT onto Highway 1 (Shoreline Highway).

8.8   Turn RIGHT at the Pelican Inn toward Muir Beach.

9.0   End of the ride at Muir Beach.

Further Information

Mt. Tamalpais Pantoll Ranger Station: (415) 388-2070
Muir Woods National Monument: (415) 388-2595

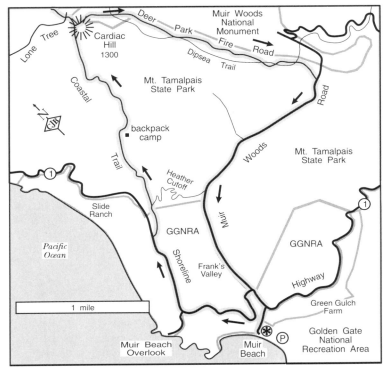

Ride No. 40

Downhill cruising along Deer Park Fire Road.

41 Olema

Bolinas Ridge and Point Reyes

Region: *North Bay*	**Total Distance:** *27 miles*
Difficulty Rating: *Difficult*	**Off-Road Distance:** *16 miles*
Skill Level: *Advanced*	**Riding Time:** *3-4 hours*
Elevation Gain: *2300 feet*	**Total Calories:** *1400*

About the Ride

Running roughly parallel to Highway 1 in a north-south direction, the Bolinas Ridge Trail skirts along the top of the inland mountain range stretching from Bolinas north to Olema, near Point Reyes. Expansive views of Bolinas Lagoon in the south and Tomales Bay in the north make the trail one of the more beautiful ones to ride in the North Bay Area.

Just west of Bolinas Ridge Trail, across Highway 1, lies Point Reyes National Seashore. While Point Reyes has only a small number of trails on which bikes are permitted, there is one trail, Olema Valley Trail, running parallel to Highway 1, which can be conveniently tied in with the Bolinas Ridge Trail to make a challenging and interesting loop.

The route starts in Olema, near the turn-off for Point Reyes visitor center and park headquarters. After heading south on Highway 1 for about 4 miles, you will then turn into the Five Brooks parking area to get on the trail through Point Reyes National Seashore. From there, Olema Valley Trail will take you through the inland forests and some open meadows along a very challenging single-track. Olema Valley Trail comes back out to Highway 1 just north of Bolinas. You will then follow Highway 1 south to Fairfax-Bolinas Road and then climb to the top of Bolinas Ridge along the road. The trailhead for Bolinas Ridge Trail is at the top of the hill. After some early ups and downs, Bolinas Ridge Trail will take you on a steady descent through pastures and woods until it terminates at Sir Francis Drake Boulevard. The return into Olema is along this road.

Olema Valley Trail is narrow, often overgrown and usually quite bumpy. Bolinas Ridge Trail, on the other hand, is a wide fire road leading through pastures with grazing cattle. While the trail is a public one, numerous livestock gates require you to lift your bike over a fence in order to get through.

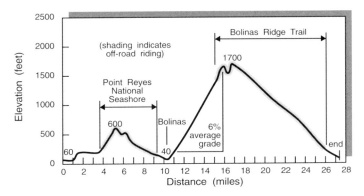

Starting Point

Start the ride in Olema at the intersection of Sir Francis Drake Boulevard and Highway 1. To get there, take Highway 101 and get off at the exit for Sir Francis Drake Boulevard. Follow Sir Francis Drake Boulevard west all the way to its end at Highway 1 in Olema.

Mile Markers

0.0   Proceed SOUTH on Highway 1 away from Olema.

3.6   Turn RIGHT into Five Brooks area of Point Reyes National Seashore and continue to the parking area at the end of the road.

3.9   Proceed toward Five Brooks Trail, but turn LEFT onto a small unmarked trail just out of the parking lot. This will lead to Olema Valley Trail.

4.0   Bear LEFT at the trail split.

5.3   Bolema Trail intersection on the right side.

6.6   Bear RIGHT at the trail split to stay on Olema Valley Trail.

8.9   Texeira Trail intersection on the right side.

9.4   End of Olema Valley Trail. Turn RIGHT onto Highway 1.

10.6 Turn LEFT onto Fairfax-Bolinas Road and begin climbing.

15.1 Turn LEFT onto Bolinas Ridge Trail at the top of the hill. Trail is well-marked with a prominent gate.

16.9 High point — 1700 feet.

19.8 Randall Trail intersection on the left side.

20.9 Shafter Fire Road intersection on the right side.

24.7 Bear LEFT at trail split to continue toward Sir Francis Drake Boulevard — Jewell Trail branches to the right.

26.1 Turn LEFT at the end of the trail onto Sir Francis Drake Boulevard.

27.3 End of the ride back in Olema.

Further Information

Point Reyes National Seashore: (415) 663-1092
Marin Municipal Water District —
     Sky Oaks Ranger Station: (415) 459-5267

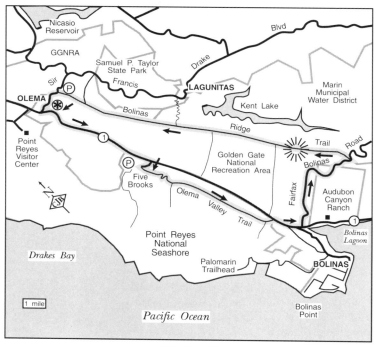

Ride No. 41

42 Olema

Point Reyes National Seashore

Region: *North Bay*
Difficulty Rating: *Easy*
Skill Level: *Beginner*
Elevation Gain: *500 feet*

Total Distance: *6 miles*
Off-Road Distance: *6 miles*
Riding Time: *1 hour*
Total Calories: *350*

About the Ride

Point Reyes National Seashore has but a few trails legal for bikes. The vast majority of the park is dedicated to hikers and equestrians. This ride is a great opportunity to combine an easy bike ride with a hike. Bring along a snack (or a banquet, for that matter) and get the complete Point Reyes experience. Be sure to wear shoes that will allow you to walk comfortably.

The ride is quite simple, following directly away from the visitor center along Bear Valley Trail. The trail is shady, wide, and smooth, and usually is quite cool, even in the summer months. Although there is a slight hill to get over, the grade is small and can be handled by just about anyone.

At the end of Bear Valley Trail is a rack for storing bikes. Be sure to bring a lock to safely secure your bike, if you plan to do the hike. There are several trails which intersect at the end of the bike path, so you can pick your own hiking option. Two of them are offered as suggestions: an easy out-and-back to the shoreline and a more difficult loop.

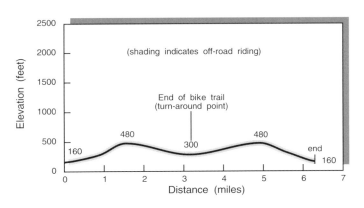

Starting Point

Start the ride in Olema at the park headquarters and visitor center for Point Reyes National Seashore. To get there, take Highway 101 and get off at the exit for Sir Francis Drake Boulevard. Follow Sir Francis Drake Boulevard west all the way to its end at Highway 1 in Olema. Turn right on Highway 1 for about 0.1 miles and then turn left onto Bear Valley Road. Follow the signs to the visitor center, where there is information about Point Reyes.

Mile Markers

0.0 Proceed to the end of the road going by the visitor center, where the trailhead for Bear Valley Trail is located. Continue on Bear Valley Trail.

0.2 Sky Trail intersection on the right side.

0.8 Meadow Trail intersection on the right side.

1.5 Divide Meadow — high point of the ride — Old Pine Trail intersection on the right side.

3.2 End of the bicycle trail. Bike racks allow you to lock your bikes and hike along any of the several trails intersecting at this point. When you are done, return back to the visitor center along Bear Valley Trail, the way you came.

Easy hike: Out-and-back along Bear Valley Trail to Arch Rock — about 1.8 miles, round trip.

Longer hike: Loop consisting of Baldy Trail, Sky Trail, Coast Trail, and Glen Trail — about 5.6 miles total.

Further Information

Point Reyes National Seashore: (415) 663-1092

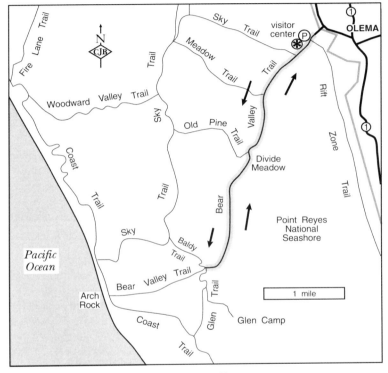

Ride No. 42

43 Lagunitas

Samuel P. Taylor State Park and Bolinas Ridge Loop

Region: *North Bay*
Difficulty Rating: *Moderate*
Skill Level: *Intermediate*
Elevation Gain: *1200 feet*

Total Distance: *14 miles*
Off-Road Distance: *12 miles*
Riding Time: *3 hours*
Total Calories: *900*

About the Ride

The redwood groves, along the tranquil Papermill Creek in Samuel P. Taylor State Park, and the grassy slopes of the Bolinas Ridge, just to the west and high above, highlight this ride.

The route begins just inside the park entrance on Sir Francis Drake Boulevard, slightly west of the town of Lagunitas. It initially follows the access road northward through the park and then continues along the paved bike trail running parallel to the creek. The peace and quiet and the beauty of the majestic redwoods provide a soothing backdrop for this gentle warm-up.

At the end of the bike trail, a little over three miles into the ride, the warm-up is over as you get on Sir Francis Drake Boulevard and climb the hill to the trailhead for Bolinas Ridge Trail. A wide fire road, Bolinas Ridge Trail has some wonderful views of Point Reyes to the west. The slope isn't steep, but the trail climbs steadily for about five miles to the junction with Shafter Bridge Fire Road, at an elevation of 1,360 feet. Shafter Bridge Road descends quite steeply along a winding route and ends up, fittingly, at Shafter Bridge, back on Sir Francis Drake Boulevard. The ride back follows Sir Francis Drake Boulevard and then along a gravel bike path running through the park.

While the climb along Bolinas Ridge Trail is not terribly steep, the numerous livestock gates along the way will require you to dismount and lift your bike over the fence. The descent on Shafter Bridge Trail is quite steep, on the other hand, and you may actually need to stop to rest your hands. You need to brake hard nearly all the way down.

Starting Point

Begin the ride at Samuel P. Taylor State Park. To get there, take Highway 101 to southern Marin County and get off at Sir Francis Drake Boulevard. Follow Sir Francis Drake Boulevard about 16 miles west to the park entrance. Begin the ride just past the park entrance.

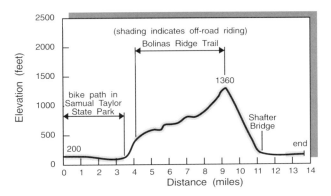

Mile Markers

0.0 Proceed into the park along the road coming from the park entrance.

0.1 Cross over bridge and turn RIGHT at the end of the entrance road onto the main road leading through the park.

1.2 Continue past the gate onto the paved bike path.

3.4 Just before the road undercrossing, turn LEFT on a gravel path leading out to the Sir Francis Drake Boulevard and turn LEFT on it. Follow the road up the hill.

4.1 At the top of the hill, turn LEFT onto Bolinas Ridge Trail.

5.2 First of many livestock gates.

5.5 Bear RIGHT to stay on Bolinas Ridge Trail (Jewell Trail branches to the left).

9.3 Turn LEFT onto unmarked fire road. This is Shafter Bridge Trail. Prepare for a steep descent. (If you get to Randall Trail intersection on the right side, you went about a mile beyond the Shafter Trail turn-off.)

10.7 Turn LEFT onto gravel trail at the bottom.

11.2 Turn LEFT onto Sir Francis Drake Boulevard at Shafter Bridge at the end of the trail.

12.5 Cross bridge on the main road and then look for the bike path on the right side. Turn RIGHT and then LEFT to get on the main bike path.

13.3 Back on the paved road in the park, turn RIGHT and cross bridge toward the park entrance.

13.4 End of the ride back at the start point.

Further Information

Samuel P. Taylor State Park: (415) 488-9897
Marin Municipal Water District —
    Sky Oaks Ranger Station: (415) 459-5267

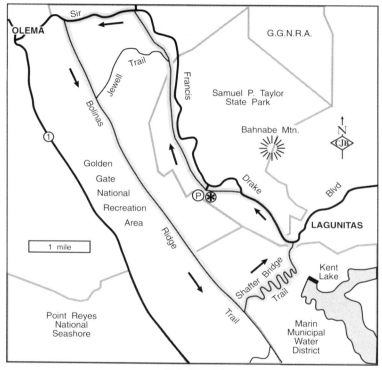

Ride No. 43

44   Santa Rosa
Annadel State Park — Lake Ilsanjo

Region: *North Bay*
Difficulty Rating: *Easy*
Skill Level: *Intermediate*
Elevation Gain: *800 feet*

Total Distance: *7 miles*
Off-Road Distance: *7 miles*
Riding Time: *1-2 hours*
Total Calories: *500*

About the Ride

Just east of Santa Rosa, on the northern fringe of the Bay Area about 60 miles north of San Francisco, lies Annadel State Park. Established as a state park in 1971, it encompasses about 5,000 acres of diverse habitats for the wildlife which can be found there. Ranging from deep redwood forests to open meadows filled with majestic live oaks and manzanita, the continuously changing scenery of Annadel is one of its main features for the mountain bike explorer.

This relatively easy ride into the park will take you out of the main parking lot along shady Warren P. Richardson Trail. While the trail climbs immediately, rising from about 400 feet in elevation to 900 feet, the grade is a gradual one. Louis Trail is a single-track that cuts through some heavy growth and leads to North Burma Trail. Slow going is the order of the day along North Burma Trail, since it is usually very bumpy. Live Oak Trail, by contrast, leads smoothly through a pleasant open meadow to Rough Go Trail and, finally, Lake Ilsanjo. At the lake, be sure to stop at the dam and to enjoy the views. Lake Ilsanjo takes its name from a combination of those of the previous owners of the property, Ilsa and Joseph Coney. The route continues around the lake along Canyon Trail until it meets up once again with Warren P. Richardson Trail for the return back.

There is one main climb, a fairly easy one, to Lake Ilsanjo. After that, it is mostly flat with a final downhill to the starting point. The trails are generally quite smooth with the exception of North Burma Trail, which can be expected to be quite bumpy with grapefruit-sized rocks. The trails are well-marked, but the main intersection at the 2.6 mile mark can be a bit confusing. Watch for equestrians and hikers and always stay off trails forbidden for bicyclists.

Starting Point

To get to Annadel State Park, take Highway 101 to Santa Rosa and get off at the exit for Highway 12. Follow Highway 12 east as it winds its way through Santa Rosa. After about 4 miles, turn right onto Mission

Boulevard and then left onto Montgomery Drive. Follow Montgomery Drive for another 1.5 miles to Channel Drive. Park in the lot at the very end of Channel Drive.

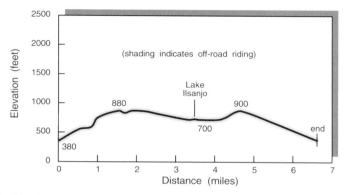

Mile Markers

0.0 Proceed into the park on Warren P. Richardson Trail.

0.8 Two Quarry Trail intersection on the left side.

1.5 Turn RIGHT onto Louis Trail.

1.9 Turn RIGHT onto bumpy North Burma Trail.

2.3 Turn LEFT onto Live Oak Trail.

2.6 Continue directly STRAIGHT ahead on Rough Go Trail. There are six trails merging together at this point, so be sure to take the one straight ahead.

3.3 Bear LEFT to stay on Rough Go Trail and continue across the dam for Lake Ilsanjo.

3.5 Continue STRAIGHT at the intersection with Canyon Trail on the right side.

3.8 Continue STRAIGHT at the intersection with Steve's S Trail on the right side.

4.1 Turn RIGHT onto Warren P. Richardson Trail.

4.5 Continue STRAIGHT at the intersection with South Burma Trail on the right side.

4.7 Bear RIGHT to stay on Warren P. Richardson Trail.

5.9 Two Quarry Trail intersection on the right side.

6.7 End of the ride back at the parking lot.

Further Information

Annadel State Park: (707) 539-3911.

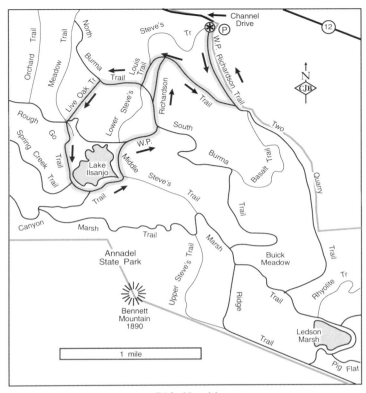

Ride No. 44

Lake Ilsanjo in Annadel State Park.

45 Santa Rosa
Annadel State Park — Ledson Marsh

Region: *North Bay*
Difficulty Rating: *Moderate*
Skill Level: *Intermediate*
Elevation Gain: *1300 feet*

Total Distance: *14 miles*
Off-Road Distance: *14 miles*
Riding Time: *2-3 hours*
Total Calories: *900*

About the Ride

Just outside of Santa Rosa, about 60 miles north of San Francisco, lies one of the most popular mountain bike destinations for the North Bay. Annadel State Park, encompassing some 5,000 acres of redwoods, oaks, manzanita, and scrub brush, has terrain and scenery to both inspire and to challenge. While the elevations don't match those of the higher coastal mountains and the trails aren't terribly steep, the indigenous rocks found in the soil make the going quite rough in many places. Tricky climbs and bone-jarring descents present the main challenges in Annadel. The rewards are the diverse scenery and the stunning views.

This ride covers a fairly complete tour of the park and includes loops around both Lake Ilsanjo and the Ledson Marsh. The route leads from the main parking lot uphill along smooth and shady W.P. Richardson Trail. A short stretch of single-track on Louis Trail is followed by a bumpy section along North Burma Trail and a smooth cruise through a pleasant meadow along Live Oak Trail. Rough Go Trail leads to tranquil Lake Ilsanjo and a convenient stopping point at the dam. A short distance on Canyon Trail leads to the main climb in the ride, first on bumpy Marsh Trail and then on Ridge Trail.

The ride around Ledson Marsh is flat and smooth. The best time to view the wildlife in the marsh is in the spring after the winter rains. The marsh normally dries up in late-summer, but is always a peaceful place to experience. The return trip follows once again along Marsh Trail and then the fun begins on the hairy descent along rugged South Burma Trail. Even shock absorbers don't completely absorb the pounding your hands are bound to take on this section. The final part of the ride back to the starting point again follows W.P. Richardson Trail.

Starting Point

To get to Annadel State Park, take Highway 101 to Santa Rosa and get off at the exit for Highway 12. Follow Highway 12 east as it winds its way through Santa Rosa. After about 4 miles, turn right onto Mission Boulevard and then left onto Montgomery Drive. Follow Montgomery

Drive for another 1.5 miles to Channel Drive. Park in the lot at the very end of Channel Drive.

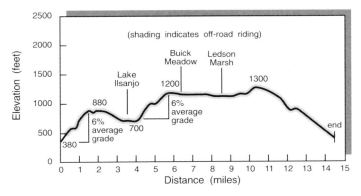

Mile Markers

0.0 Proceed into the park on Warren P. Richardson Trail.

0.8 Two Quarry Trail intersection on the left side.

1.5 Turn RIGHT onto Louis Trail.

1.9 Turn RIGHT onto bumpy North Burma Trail.

2.3 Turn LEFT onto Live Oak Trail.

2.6 Continue directly STRAIGHT ahead on Rough Go Trail. There are six trails merging together at this point, so be sure to take the one straight ahead.

3.3 Bear LEFT to stay on Rough Go Trail and continue across the dam for Lake Ilsanjo.

3.5 Turn RIGHT onto Canyon Trail.

4.1 Turn LEFT onto bumpy Marsh Trail and begin climbing.

6.1 Bear RIGHT to stay on Marsh Trail at Buick Meadow (South Burma Trail is on the left.)

6.4 Turn RIGHT onto Ridge Trail.

7.8 Turn LEFT onto Marsh Trail.

8.1 Continue STRAIGHT at Pig Flat Trail intersection on the right and wind around the marsh.

9.1 Bear LEFT to stay on Marsh Trail at the intersection with Two Quarry Trail on the right side.

9.5 Ridge Trail intersection on the left side.

9.8 Turn RIGHT onto South Burma Trail.

12.2 Turn RIGHT onto Warren P. Richardson Trail.

12.4 Bear RIGHT to stay on Warren P. Richardson Trail.

13.6 Two Quarry Trail intersection on the right side.

14.4 End of the ride back at the parking lot.

Further Information

Annadel State Park: (707) 539-3911.

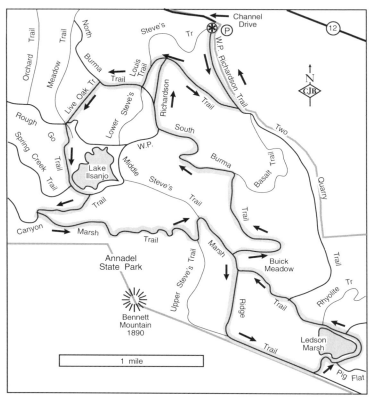

Ride No. 45

Buick Meadow in Annadel State Park.

APPENDIX

RIDES BY DIFFICULTY LEVEL

Ride No.	Ride Name	Miles	Elevation	Page No.
Easy Rides				
7.	Los Gatos Creek Trail	17	300	30
8.	The Loma Prieta Earthquake Epicenter	9	120	33
12.	Henry Cowell Redwoods State Park	8	700	45
15.	The Arastradero Preserve	5	500	57
18.	Mountain View Shoreline Park	20	40	66
21.	Old Haul Road	16	800	75
29.	Coyote Hills Regional Park	15	100	100
30.	Morgan Territory	7	600	103
42.	Point Reyes National Seashore	6	500	141
44.	Annadel State Park – Lake Ilsanjo	7	800	147
Moderate Rides				
2.	St. Joseph's Hill	6	700	15
9.	The Forest of Nisene Marks and Sand Point Overlook	22	1500	36
13.	Big Basin State Park	16	1500	48
14.	Wilder Ranch State Historic Preserve	18	1600	52
17.	Fremont Older Open Space Preserve	8	1300	63
19.	Sweeney Ridge	12	1600	69
22.	Russian Ridge Open Space Preserve	11	1300	78
23.	Skyline Ridge Open Space Preserve	7	1200	81
24.	Saratoga Gap and Long Ridge Preserves	10	900	84
27.	Redwood Regional Park	10	1200	94
33.	Tilden Park and Wildcat Canyon	17	1700	112
37.	Tennessee Valley and Muir Beach Loop	11	1700	126
38.	Mt. Tamalpais East Peak Loop	12	1500	129
39.	Mt. Tamalpais Watershed — Lakes Loop	11	1100	132
40.	Mt. Tamalpais and Muir Woods	9	1300	135
43.	Samuel P. Taylor State Park and Bolinas Ridge Loop	14	1200	144
45.	Annadel State Park – Ledson Marsh	14	1300	150
Difficult Rides				
1.	Grant Ranch County Park	16	1900	11
3.	Sierra Azul Open Space Preserve #1	12	2300	18
4.	Sierra Azul Open Space Preserve #2	13	2700	21

Vasona Lake along the Los Gatos Creek Trail.

MOUNTAIN BIKING TIPS

Benefit from the experience of others by familiarizing yourself with these simple tips for better and safer cycling.

General Rules of Cycling on Public Roads

1. Always ride on the right side of the road and never ride against the flow of traffic.
2. Always ride in a single file.
3. Signal when you are turning or slowing down in order to allow the rider behind you to prepare for the same and to allow cars to know what you are doing.
4. Never ride on freeways. This is simply too dangerous.
5. Cross railroad tracks and cattle guards at right angles to the rails.
6. In the rain or on wet surfaces, ride slower and more cautiously than you normally would. Remember that not only are the trails muddy and the roads slippery, but your brakes often have less stopping power when they are wet.
7. Avoid night riding.
8. Never assume that a hiker, equestrian, or another cyclist will give you the right of way.
9. When making a left turn in traffic, ride assertively, but give clear signals. Be sure to wave appreciatively when another vehicle gives you clearance.
10. Always stop at red lights and stop signs. Cyclists have no special privileges.
11. Signal to trailing cyclists the presence of debris or potholes in the road, either of which can be difficult for them to see.

Rules for Off-Road Riding

1. Know the rules for the area in which you are riding. Always stay on the trails intended for bikes. Resist the urge to explore in areas where bikes are not permitted.
2. Yield to equestrians. Horses may spook when a bicycle appears suddenly.
3. Yield to hikers.
4. Riders going downhill should yield to those going uphill on narrow trails. It is much harder to get off and then on again when going uphill.
5. Always be courteous. Nothing is worse for the sport than ill-will created by impolite actions.
6. Look ahead on the trail to anticipate encounters with others.

7. Avoid contact with plant life along the trails. Poison oak is very common in northern California and can be a very unpleasant experience.

8. Carry maps at all times. Getting lost is no fun.

9. Do not leave any trash behind.

10. When you stop to take a break or catch your breath, be sure to get completely off the trail and out of the way of other riders.

11. Don't talk too loudly while you are riding. This disturbs the natural quiet of nature and can ruin the experience for others.

12. As you overtake another rider or hiker on the trail, announce your approach. As you pass by, be sure to say hello and to thank them for allowing you to pass.

Mountain Biking Techniques

1. A properly adjusted seat height will ensure your comfort and will help to avoid knee injuries. The correct height will result in a slight bend in the knee when the leg is in its fully extended position to the lower of the two pedals.

2. Be familiar with gear shifting so you can anticipate hill climbs and shift *before* you need to. It can be difficult to shift when there is a lot of pressure on the pedals and the chain can come off under these conditions. Always shift while you are pedaling.

3. If your bike is equipped with toe clips, try pulling up on the pedals, as well as pushing down. This uses different muscles and can give you better efficiency for long rides.

4. When riding on fire trails, it is common to encounter steep downhill sections. To safely deal with these, stop and lower your seat before you descend. This lowers your center of gravity and also allows you to dismount quickly.

5. Use your front brake more than your rear one on steep descents. There is much more weight on your front wheel going downhill. Using your rear brake can cause unnecessary skids and force you to lose control.

6. On a trail which is uneven on the left and right sides, dismount to the side of the trail which is the highest.

7. When riding with a group, it is both safe and polite to regroup periodically.

8. Don't focus on a particular rock or hazard ahead of you. If you do, you will tend to steer toward it.

9. After a crash or wipeout, don't be overly aggressive when you resume riding. Re-build your confidence slowly.

10. Avoid the temptation to stand in order to climb steep sections. This reduces your rear wheel traction and doesn't help very

much. Instead, get into a low enough gear, lower your body to put some weight on the front wheel, and slug it out.

Tips on Equipment

1. Always carry a spare tube, patch kit, tire pump, and tools. Allen wrenches and a chain tool can also come in handy in unusual situations.
2. Be prepared to fix your own bike. Don't count on others to do this for you.
3. Check tire pressure, seat height, brakes, and shifters *before* you begin each ride.
4. Recommended tire pressure is usually indicated on the side of the tire. Mountain biking over rough or soft surfaces often works better when the tires are slightly deflated. Road riding is easiest with fully inflated tires.
5. Carry adequate water supplies. There may not be water available on the trails.
6. A handlebar pack or panniers are convenient for carrying extra clothing or snacks.
7. Toe clips give you better riding efficiency on long rides, but mountain bikes are probably better without them. You often need to dismount quickly in rough terrain and toe clips can make this difficult to do.

Appropriate Clothing

1. Protect your head with a helmet.
2. Gloves are not necessary, but long rides without them can cause blisters or blood circulation problems.
3. It is good to carry a lightweight windbreaker, even on warm days. High altitudes are often colder than you anticipate.
4. Long pants and winter gloves are usually necessary for rides in the cold months.
5. Some sort of eyewear is strongly recommended. Either cycling goggles or sunglasses will provide protection from dirt, debris, and insects, as well as screen your eyes from the harmful effects of the sun's ultraviolet rays.

ABOUT THE AUTHOR

After a 25-year career as an electronics engineer, Conrad Boisvert retired in 1990 and began writing. This is his first book on mountain biking and follows his earlier road biking books, *South Bay Bike Trails*, *San Francisco Peninsula Bike Trails,* and *East Bay Bike Trails*.

Born in New Jersey in 1943, his residence in northern California since 1972 has fulfilled his desire to live where there is a wide variety of readily available outdoor activities. Besides cycling, his interests include tennis, basketball, hiking, and snow skiing. He is the father of three grown children and currently resides in the Willow Glen area of San Jose.

The author.

THE BAY AREA BIKE TRAILS SERIES

East Bay Bike Trails by Conrad J. Boisvert, 1992. $11.95. Somewhat sheltered from coastal fog and ocean winds, the East Bay is often warmer than other regions in the Bay Area. Extending from the Carquinez Strait south to Fremont, interesting bike routes take you through heavily wooded hills above Oakland and Berkeley, orchards and farms around Brentwood, unique and eerie windmills in Livermore, the wetlands around Newark, and dramatic Mount Diablo in Danville.

San Francisco Peninsula Bike Trails by Conrad J. Boisvert, 1991. $11.95. Few areas can compare with the spectacular San Francisco Peninsula, which encompasses the wooded foothills around Woodside, dense redwood forests in the Santa Cruz mountains, and remote country roads along the rugged Pacific coastline so characteristic of Northern California.

South Bay Bike Trails by Conrad J. Boisvert, 1990. $11.95. Although better known for its high-technology image, the South Bay is a cyclist's paradise, once you head out into the surrounding countryside. From San Jose south to Gilroy, picturesque rides take you through ranchlands around Morgan Hill, dense redwood forests in the Santa Cruz mountains, and the coastal wetlands of the Elkhorn Slough. Heading south along the Pacific coast brings you to the famous seaside resorts and beaches of Santa Cruz and Capitola.

Marin County Bike Trails by Phyllis L. Neumann, 1989. $11.95. North across the Golden Gate Bridge, Marin County combines exquisite natural beauty with sophisticated elegance to give you spectacular views, rugged cliffs, natural beaches, well-developed parks, rural farmlands, tiny hidden towns and Mt. Tamalpais. A specially designed bike route from Petaluma to the Golden Gate Bridge is also included.

Sonoma County Bike Trails by Phyllis L. Neumann, 1978. Revised Edition, 1990. $11.95. Less than an hour's drive north from San Francisco brings you to tranquil country roads, gently rolling farmlands, towering redwoods, lush vineyards, local wineries, the Russian River, and the Pacific coastline. A specially designed bike route from Cloverdale to Petaluma is also included.

Each book contains easy-to-challenging self-guided bike rides, complete with detailed maps, elevation profiles, and photographs.

Copies may be ordered directly from Penngrove Publications. Please add $1.50 for shipping and handling. California residents add 7½% sales tax for each book ordered.

Penngrove Publications
P.O. Box 1017
Penngrove, CA 94951